COWBOY METAPHYSICS:
ETHICS AND DEATH IN WESTERNS

COWBOY METAPHYSICS:
ETHICS AND DEATH IN WESTERNS

· Peter A. French ·

ROWMAN & LITTLEFIELD PUBLISHERS, INC.
Lanham • Boulder • New York • Oxford

ROWMAN & LITTLEFIELD PUBLISHERS, INC.

Published in the United States of America
by Rowman & Littlefield Publishers, Inc.
4720 Boston Way, Lanham, Maryland 20706

12 Hid's Copse Road
Cummor Hill, Oxford OX2 9JJ, England

British Cataloging in Publication Information Available

Library of Congress Cataloging-in-Publication Data

French, Peter A.
   Cowboy metaphysics : ethics and death in westerns
/ Peter A. French
        p. cm.
   Includes bibliographical references and index.
   ISBN 0–8476–8670-1 (cloth : alk. paper). — ISBN 0–8476–8671-X
(paper : alk. paper)
   1. Western films—Moral and ethical aspects.
PN1995.9.W4F69 1997
791.43/6278'21—dc20   97-036097
                                                             CIP

ISBN 0–8476–8670-1 (cloth : alk. paper)
ISBN 0–8476–8671-X (pbk. : alk. paper)

Printed in the United States of America

For SANDRA

CONTENTS

PREFACE

For as far back as I can remember, I have enjoyed watching Westerns. I used to go to a shabby little neighborhood movie theater, pay fourteen cents, and watch a double bill where at least one of the features was a Western. When a major Western such as *Red River, High Noon,* or *Shane* was released, I thought nothing of skipping school and riding the streetcar downtown to watch the film in one of the opulent theaters. My first experience with a television set was in the late 1940s, and the first images I saw on the tube were that of Sunset Carson and his horse galloping along the sagebrush trail. I was in high school and then college in the period of the Western's greatest cultural impact, the fifties, so I could hardly escape its influence. In short, I grew up with Westerns, grew old with them, and hope the relationship ends there.

I find the Western film genre ethically intriguing both within the cultural context in which it appears and has enjoyed popularity, because it so thoroughly rejects the world view of that culture, and within itself. This book is my attempt to philosophically examine some of the underlying positions on which the ethics of the Western are constructed. I am especially interested in what lessons might be learned from these movies about the relationship between one's conception of death and the moral position one adopts. This book is definitely not intended as film criticism. I have little or no interest in contrasting the films with each other or with attacking or defending this or that director's use of characters, images, and basic plotlines. The films, for me, are a place of departure in the process of trying to construct what might eventually become an alternative to the standard view of what it is ethical to do and not do. I do not pretend for a minute that the way I will be "reading" the films captures the intent of their creators. In fact, I could not care less.

For a number of years I have been telling people that I wanted to write a book about the ethics of Westerns. The general response was that there could not be much to say after white and black hats were identified. I tried to explain that I was not interested in the B Westerns of Roy Rogers, Gene

Autry, Johnny Mack Brown, Hopalong Cassidy, and their cohorts. I wanted to focus on the great films, the A films, that define the genre. Most nodded and humored me, but told me to get on with other projects. Finally I finished or set aside those other projects and got to work on the Westerns. A major impetus for my doing so was the appearance in 1992 of Jane Tompkins's important book, *West of Everything.*[1] I had purchased her book when it first came out and had carted it around with me on a number of trips, hoping to find the time to read it. I was in Taiwan to give lectures in the summer of 1994 and had to spend about eight hours in Chiang Kai-shek Airport waiting for a flight to Los Angeles. I dug Tompkins's book out of my bag and read it through in the Singapore Airlines lounge. I am sure there is something deeply ironic in that. When I finished, having enjoyed and benefited from her work, despite frequent disagreements, I decided that the time had come for me, as a philosopher, to take on the Western. I arranged to offer an "Ethics in Westerns" seminar and started seriously reviewing the films.

Two matters of clarification: (1) By "Westerns" throughout this book I specifically refer to major movies set in the American West that are about cowboys, gunslingers, etc. I exclude films primarily about American Indian tribes, the cavalry, and survival in the wilderness. The paradigm Westerns for my purposes are such films as *Shane, Red River, The Man Who Shot Liberty Valance, High Noon, McCabe and Mrs. Miller, Will Penny, Monte Walsh, The Missouri Breaks, The Shootist, Pale Rider,* and *Unforgiven.* Some films in which American Indian tribes are depicted will also qualify because the main plot conflicts are not between whites and Indians, but rather between and within what I will call the "westerners." In that category are *Stagecoach, The Searchers, Hombre,* and *The Outlaw Josey Wales.*

(2) I will *not* be talking about the historical western American experience. I am interested in a genre of film in the movies. Whether or not the West really was "won" in the way depicted in the films is of no interest to me. The director Sam Peckinpah said: "I don't make documentaries. The facts about the siege of Troy, of the duel between Hector and Achilles and all the rest of it, are a hell of a lot less interesting to me than what Homer makes of it. And the mere facts tend to obscure the truth anyway."[2] Jon Tuska goes to great lengths to criticize Westerns because they are not factual reproductions of the history of the American West. He also bemoans that "All I can do is express my regret that an ostensible entertainment medium should have so consistently reinforced the notion that murder is frequently the only solution to social problems and a prerequisite for entering upon a better life; that an entire race of people can be virtually wiped out only to be regarded as 'mythological' by filmmakers and film critics alike . . ."[3]

What would Tuska say of the epics of Homer? Did it really happen that way? Who cares? Well, obviously Tuska does and so, apparently, do a number of historians. But I don't. In this book, I am interested in what is on the screen, not in what ought to be there if only some more "sensitive guy," one more dedicated to historical accuracy and contemporary social causes than John Ford or Anthony Mann or Clint Eastwood, had been behind the camera.

I will not be criticizing the way Westerns portray American Indians or blacks or how they use (or abuse) animals. Suffice it to say that until recently Westerns, and films in general, have done an abysmal job on all of these counts. I do not particularly care, however, that John Ford used Navahos to play the part of Cheyenne or Apaches. I do cringe when Jeff Chandler, or someone like him from Brooklyn, plays a war chief or Debra Paget is cast as a Sioux woman. But I have restricted myself to the Westerns that do not particularly feature minorities, and, in any event, I will not be using the opportunity to discuss the issues I want to raise in Westerns to reiterate those well-worn, though clearly appropriate, criticisms of the way Hollywood, until quite recently, represented minorities.

I have tried to be accurate in my use of dialogue from the films. I have not trusted my memory. I have also not used the scripts of the films because I am not concerned with what some writer wrote or wanted the actors to say. My interest is in what actually appears in the final cut of the film. I have worked from the films themselves. Most of the films I discuss are now available on videotape. I urge the reader to view them.

I have noticed while reading some of the books written about Westerns and other film genres that their authors get a surprising number of things wrong. A friend of mine who has written about another genre once told me that he trusts his memory of the films, and if he mixes them up once in a while, that mix up may also be important for what he is saying about the films. I remain puzzled about his response. I have tried to avoid outright errors, which, no doubt, on some evenings has driven my wife up the walls as I run and rerun certain segments of a film. Factual errors about the films pepper many of the books on Westerns. For example, Tompkins tells us that *High Noon* begins in church.[4] Anyone who has seen the film should remember that it does not. It begins on a hill outside of Hadleyville where the Miller gang is gathering. Then it follows the gang into town. People are shown entering a church as the gang rides by and a Mexican woman crosses herself when she sees the gang. Perhaps Tompkins is thinking of the wedding of Will Kane and Amy Fowler that we next see. The wedding, however, is held in the marshal's office and is conducted by the justice of the peace, a fact that is of no little importance later when Kane enters the church to ask for help against the Miller gang. Tompkins also tells us that "*Cowboy* posits a world . . . without ideas, without institutions, without what is commonly recognized as culture."[5] She must have forgotten that the lead character in the film, the cattle drive foreman and rancher Tom Reese (played by Glenn Ford), comes to Chicago not only to sell his cattle, but to attend the opera. Much is made of that fact in the film. She also misquotes the dialogue in the films. For example, she alters Tom Reese's funeral eulogy in *Cowboy*. More egregiously, however, she tells us that the search in *The Searchers* goes on for seven years when it took five years.

I want to thank the students in my seminar on Ethics and Westerns, and especially Frank Barnes, for their frequent insights. They helped me formulate some of the positions I take in the book. My colleagues at The Ethics Center and in the Philosophy Department at the University of South Florida, especially Professors Peggy DesAutels, Margaret Urban Walker, and Joanne Waugh, provided helpful comments. Our disagreements were as stimulating as our agreements. My daughter, Dr. Shannon French, was most helpful and provided some valuable references. My wife, Sandra, offered valuable editorial suggestions for the book and watched all of the films with me, many more than once. It is a joy that she also loves Westerns and the West. If this book is accessible to those without technical philosophical backgrounds, but does not miss its intended philosophical targets, it is in large measure due to her prodding me for clarity. I found most useful those discussions I had with audiences that listened to parts of the book while it was in progress. I want to express my thanks to those at the North American Society for Social Philosophy meetings in Maine in the summer of 1995, various groups in Florida, and my National Endowment for the Humanities Summer Seminar group in Colorado for their comments.

NOTES

1. Jane Tompkins, *West of Everything* (Oxford, 1992).
2. Sam Peckinpah, "Interview," *Playboy* (August, 1972).
3. Jon Tuska, *The American West in Film* (Westport, Conn., 1985), 264.
4. Tompkins, *West of Everything*, 35.
5. Ibid., 37.

· 1 ·

A Clash of Cares

I

In *Streets of Laredo*, Pea Eye Parker, Famous Shoes, Olin Ray, Ted Plunkert, and Brookshire are huddled around a campfire near the Rio Conchos river in northern Mexico. Brookshire is an accountant for the railroad. He has been assigned to accompany Captain Woodrow Call and his party as they attempt to track down and kill Joey Garza, a vicious murderer who has been robbing trains and killing people. Brookshire is from Brooklyn, New York. It is evening and it is cold. They use pages from Brookshire's account books to start the fire. Olin has brought the news that Plunkert's pregnant wife was raped by the sheriff back in Laredo and that she has committed suicide by swallowing rat poison. Plunkert rides off to return to Laredo, to determine if Olin's story is true. (He won't make it. He will be murdered and stripped of everything he has by Mexican bandits.) At the campfire the following conversation occurs:

> Brookshire (in tears): How far is it back?
> Pea Eye (without emotion): Back where?
> Brookshire: Back where it's not like this. People getting killed every day.
>   There's no houses, no streetcars. Back to civilization.
> Pea Eye: It's cold, ain't it?
> Olin (Nods):

The Western is about, to borrow from the title of another film based on a Larry McMurtry book, a dead man's walk,[1] or run or gallop. It is not accidental that so many of the heroes and villains of Westerns are portrayed as having a previous history in the American Civil War on the losing Confederate side. They have been defeated and lived with death and gore in a cause they, we are led to believe, saw either as their inescapable duty or as romantic. They are almost never portrayed as staunch defenders of slavery. They have much too closely identified themselves with freedom, which is,

1

apparently, how they understood the doctrine of states' rights. A song written by Jeffrey Wolfe and sung by The Horse Soldiers captures the basic theme. Its lyrics are:

> . . . Death stood at my right hand,
> I know he will stand there again . . .
> Columns lie in ruin and dust,
> The gilded halls, they're lined with rust . . .
> There's nothin' here to tie me down,
> I turn my pony's head around,
> I'm headin' for the settin' sun,
> So I'm ridin' West, I've got no regrets,
> I'll make myself forget.
> All that's lost is memories.
> So I'm ridin' West.
> I'm ridin' West.
> I'm riding, riding.[2]

Riding West is not only to ride into the unsettled frontier of mountains and valleys and deserts, especially deserts, it is to die. The ancient Egyptians called their dead "westerners." They were the people of the West, the place where everything ends, where the sun sets, where the day dies. One of the funeral dirges of the Egyptians of the period of Rameses the Great was "Let him go swiftly to the west, to the land of truth. The women of the Byblite boat weep sorely, sorely. In peace, in peace, O praised one, fare westward in peace. If it please the god, when the day changes to eternity, we shall see thee that goest now to the land where all men are one."[3] Mourners on the bank of the Nile would utter the cant, "To the West, to the West, the land of the just."[4] The gods of the dead for the Egyptians were typically referred to as "the gods of the West."[5] From the "Harpers' Songs" of the Middle Kingdom we hear:

> All our kinsmen rest in it
> Since the time of the first beginning.
> Those to be born to millions of millions,
> All of them will come to it;
> No one may linger in the land of Egypt.
> There is none who does not arrive in it.
> As to the time of deeds on earth,
> It is the occurrence of a dream;
> One says, "Welcome safe and sound,"
> To him who reaches the West.[6]

A similar identification of the West with the location of death, where life ends, is found in ancient European mythology as well. T. W. Rolleston, for example, quotes from deJubainville's *Irish Mythological Cycle*: " 'The Land of the Dead' is the western extremity of Great Britain, separated from the eastern by an impassable wall."[7]

Tompkins takes the title for her book about the elements of the Western and the Western novel from a passage in Louis L'Amour's *Hondo*. L'Amour describes the dead men of a cavalry unit that had been defeated in a battle with Apaches: ". . . the bodies of the silent men of Company C lay wide-eyed to the rain and bare-chested to the wind, but the blood and the dust washed away, and the stark features of Lieutenant Creyton C. Davis, graduate of West Point, veteran of the Civil War and the Indian wars, darling of Richmond dance floors, hero of a Washington romance, dead now in the long grass on a lonely hill, west of everything."[8]

II

Arguably, the dominant theme of the major Westerns is the conflict between what some philosophers might call "world views": the "world view" of the westerner and that of the easterner, the cowboy/gunslinger and the settler/entrepreneur/townsperson/Christian. Death is the predominant element of the westerner's world view, death of a certain kind, that is, death understood in a certain way. And from that conception of death and the West—land of death, the ethics of the westerner both emerges and is given sense. The easterner's radically different conception of death structures the world view away from which the westerner is ridin' West, but as the plots require, the easterner is forever catching up.

Though I am using the term, I am not especially comfortable with the notion of a world view, at least as it has been typically explicated. It strikes me as one of those tidy concepts philosophers create when what they think they want to talk about is a bit too messy or intractable for what passes as philosophic discourse. Martin Benjamin defines a world view, in a fairly standard way, as "a set of deeply . . . cherished beliefs about the nature and the organization of the universe and one's place in it."[9] Benjamin goes on to spell out seven elements of a world view. They include beliefs about God, about the nature and purpose of the universe and human life, about the nature and acquisition of knowledge, about the nature of human beings, about the best way to structure human relations, about the demands of morality, and about the moral standing of nonhuman animals. Although Benjamin's list of elements in a world view is probably adequate for the work the concept is supposed to do, I think he and a number of other philosophers who talk about world views and conceptual schemes are wrong in constructing world views out of beliefs in the first place. I suspect they recognize that there is something inadequate in their accounts, for usually they, like Benjamin, modify the beliefs in question. These are not just garden variety beliefs, they are "deeply cherished" or "firmly held" or "bedrock" beliefs or something of the sort. The idea is that there are beliefs and then there are deeply cherished ones. Furthermore, they can be "unarticulated (and perhaps not fully articulable)"[10] beliefs. I worry if these beliefs are not fully articulable, whether the strain is greater on the business of deeply cherishing or on believing. What is it like to deeply cherish a belief one not only does not, but cannot, fully articulate? What is it to believe it?

We should become suspicious when philosophers start working out neat packages of beliefs that persons must have and hold, even if those persons cannot articulate anything approximating the beliefs that are ascribed to them, let alone deeply cherish them. I suppose one could deeply cherish something that one could not fully articulate, for example, the feeling of pleasure at watching a mountain sunset. But I would not say that it was a belief that was being cherished. It is the feeling or even the sunset that is cherished. Perhaps more attention needs to be paid to the deeply cherishing and less to the believing with respect to world views.

I want to argue that calling the constitutive elements of a world view "beliefs," even of a special sort (the deeply cherished ones) does an injustice to what is really involved in having a world view. Some of the problems here may come from the use of the term "world view." The term suggests order and coherence, perhaps an architectonic that has been structured and designed to be a consistent and coherent set of lenses through which experience is filtered. I do not see why some elements in any particular person's or group's world view might not be at odds with others, for example, one about the existence of God and one about the purpose of human life. This should worry us if world views were just systems of propositional beliefs, for it would become evident that such a world view is incoherent and therefore difficult, if not impossible, to live by. Beliefs, because we generally think of them in terms of "beliefs *that*" rather than "beliefs *in*," are the sorts of things that are typically translated into propositional form. In that form, the temptation to measure them, at least against standards of coherence and consistency, if not truth, is almost overwhelming. But people believe *in* as well as believe *that*. Are different mental states involved? Must belief *in* always be translatable to belief *that* and take propositional form? Belief *in* is, I would think, dispositional. Believing *that*, of course, may be dispositional as well. But the dispositions involved may be discernibly different. Are the dispositions the same when it is true that I believe *that* Santa Claus exists and when I believe *in* Santa Claus? I am fairly certain that I can believe *in* Santa Claus without believing *that* Santa Claus exists. I can be said to believe *in* Santa Claus because I care about what Santa Claus, as a concept in our culture, represents. Because I believe *in* Santa Claus, because I care about Santa Claus, I am disposed to behave in certain ways at Christmastime, for example, to play a certain role in a gift-giving ritual, perhaps writing "From Santa" on certain presents I give to family members. I suppose that I might do some of the same things if I believed *that* Santa Claus exists. But there are other things I should be disposed to do, like have some explanation, when questioned about it, for his ability to transport presents to so many households over such great distances in so short a period of time.

Belief *in* gets closer to world views than belief *that*, but not close enough. What we believe *in* may reveal some of the pieces of the puzzle that is our world view, but that is because some of the things we believe *in* fall within the index of what we really care about. However, that we believe *in* something is not a sure-fire indicator of what we care about. We can believe *in* quite a number of things we could not care less about. World views, I want to argue, are constructed of what we really care about, not of what we believe *in* or believe *that*. They are constituted of cares, not beliefs.

If you care about something, it is important to you.[11] In the colloquial befitting Westerns, you "give a damn" about it. The more you care, the greater the importance for you. Care is, of course, a scalar concept. One cares a great deal, a bit, somewhat, hardly at all. And the amount of care signifies the amount of importance the object of care has for the person doing the caring. In fact, as Harry Frankfurt notes, the two concepts (caring about and importance) are intimately interrelated.[12] I only care about what is important to me, and, for something to be important to me, I must care about it. Very important = really care a lot. Less important = care less. Not important = don't give a damn.

That rather inelegant term ("give a damn") seldom finds its way into the philosophical literature. More's the pity. I want to argue that what we do and do not give a damn about (and in various degrees) lies at the very core of who we are and explains much more about what we do (our behavior) and think (our ideas) than all that philosophic discourse about world views as sets of beliefs. The ethical conflicts in Westerns are not between systems of deeply cherished beliefs; they are not so ethereal. They are between people or groups of people that care and do not care a great deal about very different things. At core, they are clashes about what is important or about the amount of importance to be attached to one thing—whether action, event, or object—rather than another.

In order to care about something, I have to guide my behavior in a particular manner or along a specific course. Caring about, Frankfurt writes, "presupposes both agency and self-consciousness."[13] To care about something is to purposefully do something with oneself. "A person who cares about something is, as it were, invested in it. He *identifies* himself with what he cares about in a sense that he makes himself vulnerable to losses and susceptible to benefits depending upon whether what he cares about is diminished or enhanced."[14] Caring about involves devotion, passion, and the structuring of a life in a way that belief (*in* or *that*) does not.

To care about something I must conceive of myself as a being with identity over time, as a being that casts itself into a future. If I think of myself as a momentary being that has no continuous existence into the future, I cannot care about anything. I can, however, have beliefs (*in* and *that*) independently of considering myself as an entity with a future. Imagine an intelligent being that comes into existence only for a single moment and then vanishes. Call this being Momentus. Suppose that Momentus is endowed with a set of beliefs at its birth. Included in that set is the belief that there exists a hell for the damnation of the sinful. Momentus believes *that* there is a Hell and Momentus might even be said to believe *in* Hell. But it would make no sense for Momentus to care about Hell, to attach any importance to Hell, at least as far as Momentus is concerned about itself. By the same token, I can want something, desire it, like it, while believing that my life "consists merely of a succession of separate moments"[15] and none of those moments is an integral element in a continuing life. The reason for this is that beliefs and desires need not have a persistence through time. Beliefs are transitory. Beliefs, by their nature, do not have to endure beyond the instance in which they are believed. They have, in Frankfurt's terms, "no inherent persistence."[16] Odd though it may sound to some, while in Salisbury Cathedral, I might believe there is a God, even one with the properties attributed to the Christian God, and then, a few moments later while walking out in the Close, believe there cannot be a God, or that a God, if one exists, could not have that set of properties. Caring about something, however, requires an extended period of time. It involves, at least some degree of, persistence of the caring self. Caring about something is not merely being moved by a momentary impulse. Though, of course, I may make the decision to care about something in an instance.

In other words, caring about something cannot be identified with the decision one makes to care about something. Momentus could make the decision to care about Hell, but Momentus cannot care about Hell.

The decision typically is momentary, the caring about takes time. I suspect that a number of us at various times in our lives decide to care about things that we never get around to caring about. For example, I am sure that at least once I decided to care about recycling aluminum soda cans. But I am afraid that anyone who casually observes my behavior on an ordinary day or examines the wastebasket in my office at the close of a workday will have ample evidence that I do not give a damn about recycling those cans. What I care about or, as in this case, what I do not care about, is, rather more important in understanding my behavior than the decisions I make, including my decisions to care about something.

I wonder if a careful look at what it is to care about things may lead us to quite a different account of weakness of will than the emphasis on decisions has produced in the literature. If the decision to recycle is crucial and I do not behave accordingly, ascribing my failure to act appropriately to *akrasia* is inviting. But, if I just do not care about recycling, is my failure to recycle, in any way, a weakness of will? Might it not simply reveal the importance I attach to recycling? It might even show a resoluteness in not recycling, though we are more likely to associate resoluteness with acting on what we really care about rather than on what we do not care about much at all. Despite momentary decisions to the contrary, if I do not care about recycling and so casually toss away aluminum cans, there is no evidence of weakness of will. You might criticize me, with justification, saying that I ought to care about recycling. You might try to persuade me to care. But if your attempts are unsuccessful, it will not be because my will is weak. That is just the sort of person I am: the sort that doesn't give a damn about recycling.

What I care about reveals more about my character and provides a better grounds for predictions of my behavior than does a listing of my decisions or my beliefs. I do not want to say that I am, that is my character in total is, to be identified with what I care about, but a great deal of who I am is a matter of what I care about. I identify myself with, in the sense that I invest (Frankfurt's term) myself in what I care about, what I give a damn about. Conflicts of duty, as Frankfurt notes, are typically due to a person's not knowing which of two alternatives he or she really cares more about or his or her caring, more or less, equally about both alternatives. The Olympic runner, Eric Liddell, whose story is told in the film *Chariots of Fire*, was caught in a conflict between a duty to his country and to his own athletic ability to run his race in the Olympics, on the one hand; and a religious duty not to do so because the race was scheduled on a Sunday and his religion forbad his participation on the Sabbath, on the other. Though he may not at first have known which of the grounds of the duties he cared most about, he resolved the conflict when he realized that he cared more about his religious than his patriotic or athletic status. Consequently, of course, no one will ever know whether Liddell actually would have beaten his arch rival Harold Abrahams in the Olympic 100 meters in 1924.

Frankfurt writes: "The fact that someone cares about a certain thing is constituted by a complex set of cognitive, affective, and volitional dispositions and states. It may sometimes be possible for a person, by making a certain choice or decision, effectively to bring it about that he cares about a certain thing or that he cares about one thing more than about another. But that depends upon conditions which do not always prevail. It certainly cannot be assumed that what a person cares about is generally under his immediate voluntary control."[17]

I leave for some other time the issue of whether a person can prevent himself or herself from caring about everything he or she does care about or the amount of caring about it he or she does. I am rather certain that we cannot help caring about certain things. Perhaps a sociobiological or Darwinian account could be put to use to identify the extent or scope of what we cannot help caring about. That is not important for my current interests. It is also the case that, not unlike falling in love, we can fall into caring about some things. I suspect that westerners do not decide to ride West. They are compelled, in some sense, to do so, to become westerners.

My correction to Benjamin's account is that a person's world view primarily comprises those things regarding the nature and organization of the universe and his or her place in it that he or she cares about, really gives a damn about. Again, however, I am uncomfortable with the elegance of the notion of "world view." It invites us to make too many assumptions about cognitive states that, typically, may be utterly unwarranted. In any event, on my account, it can make sense to say of a person that he or she believes that God exists, but does not care that God exists, and so he or she has not invested himself or herself in the existence of God. To care about the fact that God exists is to behave over time in certain ways, to adopt a way of living in which God's existence plays a significant role. Religious institutions do not just want people to believe in God's existence, they want them to care about the existence of God. Conversion has not occurred until the latter has been achieved.

III

Various types of beliefs that get incorporated as a matter of course into the accounts philosophers, including Benjamin, provide of a world view do not automatically get included in a world view if the account of a world view is given in terms of what is cared about. Benjamin tells us that "interlocking general beliefs about knowledge, reality, and values" are fitted into world views.[18] He makes it sound as if whatever is necessary to hold the elements of one's world view into a coherent bundle are themselves part of the world view. I do not see why that should be the case. Philosophers worry about the coherence of belief sets; people just live. For example, I certainly believe that the earth is round. In fact, I more than just believe it. I take it as an established piece of knowledge, something about which I am certain, that the earth is round rather than flat. I just do not care about whether or not it is round. I don't give a damn. At best, the earth's roundness is a background belief or background certainty in my life. Ludwig Wittgenstein writes: "I have a telephone conversation with New York. My friend tells me that his young trees have buds of such and such a kind. I am now convinced that his tree is . . . Am I also convinced that the earth exists? The existence of the earth is rather part of the whole picture which forms the starting point of belief in me. Does my telephone call to New York strengthen my conviction that the earth exists? Much seems fixed, and it is removed from the traffic. It is so to speak shunted onto an unused siding . . . Perhaps it was once disputed. But perhaps, for unthinkable ages, it has belonged to the scaffolding of our thoughts. (Every human being has parents.)"[19]

The shape of the earth is of no real concern to me, that is, to the life I live.

A world view, Benjamin correctly notes, is dynamically interrelated to a way of life.[20] In effect, world views govern ways of life. To say that the belief that the earth is round is a part, albeit an unarticulated part, of my world view, is gratuitous, for that belief plays no role in the governance of my way of life. If it's round, it's round. If it's flat, it's flat. I don't give a damn. My way of life is not at all "dynamically interrelated" to unarticulated beliefs (whatever they are) I may or may not have regarding the shape of the earth.

On the other hand, the shape of the earth, its roundness, could be something that some other person does really care about. According to the story, it was a crucial element in Columbus's world view. He did not just believe that the earth was round, he staked his life and reputation on it. He really cared about it, and it governed his way of life. He invested himself in it. How he lived, what he did or did not do is made intelligible because he cared about the earth being a certain shape. It was not just that he believed that the world was round, it mattered to him that it was, and it mattered in such a way that he could not forbear taking certain courses of action.

Frankfurt reminds us of Luther's famous "Here I stand, I can do no other." speech at the Diet of Worms.[21] Think also of Thomas More's refusal to swear the oath that would have saved his life. How should we understand them? In what sense could they do no other, and how could I have done the other without flinching? Apparently, I do not care about what Luther or More cared about, though I probably believe much of what they believed. Or, I do not care about it as much as they did. I care about other things much more. Why could Luther do no other? Why More? It is obvious to me, and to most other people, that Luther certainly could have done something else. He could have retracted his writings before the Diet and gotten on with whatever else he liked doing. Thomas More clearly, he could have signed the documents thrust at him by Cromwell and Cranmer, gone back to his family and his home in Chelsea, and lived out a profitable life. Where did the necessity come from that they say compelled them to stand as they did? Surely they knew the alternatives open to them. Their examiners had explained the alternatives, and Luther and More had the capacity to act other than they did. They were not under duress to continue to take their stands. If there was any duress, all of it ran the other way. But, for them the alternative actions were unthinkable, not that they could not think of them. Frankfurt uses the term "volitional necessity"[22] to refer to the kind of constraints that rendered Luther and More unable to take the alternative path of doing what their examiners wanted them to do. I want to say that they found it impossible to act in the alternative way, a way most of us would regard as the rational thing to do, because what a person cares about caring about blocks certain paths of action for that person, in the sense that the person cannot force himself or herself to take those paths.

This now sounds, however, more like an account of weakness of will than I intend. What I want to say is that one's way of life, governed by those things one cares most about, does not make one helpless when confronted with alternatives. It makes one resolute. The sort of volitional necessity that is involved is not self-disassociative. Remember that this is a matter of self-investment. (I would call it commitment, but for the overuse of that term in contexts that I worry might trivialize the point I hope I am making.) Luther does not accede to the force of his self-investment (what he cares most about) because he has not got the strength of will to overcome its influence on him. "He accedes to it because he is unwilling to oppose it and because, furthermore, his unwillingness is itself something he is unwilling to alter."[23] This is what he cares about. Luther can do no other "because he really does not want to do it."[24] In that sense, the bundle of things one cares about caring about is a vital part of one's identity, a point the playwright Robert Bolt ascribes to Thomas More as he tries to explain his stand to his daughter.[25]

IV

The better Westerns, I am going to argue, present us with a clash of cares, or world views, and ways of life. They display the conflicts that occur when those who care about the existence of God, the immortality of the human soul, obedience to divine moral commands, familial human relationships and the like confront those who could not give a damn about the existence of God, deny the immortality of man, have no interest in whether or how they will get on in a future eternal life, have invested themselves in a moral code that regards the commands of Judeo-Christian ethics as senseless, and care more about friendship relationships than marriage or familial relations. Importantly, the heroes of the films, the westerners, are of the latter, not the former, group. In other words, watching Westerns can force us to examine what it is like for someone to accede to the force of self-investment in cares that are radically foreign to those we commonly have or are urged to care about by the priesthoods of the institutions of civilized society. Most of us, after all, are easterners.[26]

The focal point of this clash of cares is death, the most seductive and necessary feature, according to Jane Tompkins, of the Western. She writes, "Death is everywhere in this genre. Not just in the shoot-outs, or the scores of bodies that pile up toward the narrative's close but, even more compellingly, in the desert landscape with which the bodies of the gunned-down eventually merge."[27] The conceptions of death held by both "camps" link up with other notions and are the grounds for volitional and affective dispositions that quite naturally conflict, creating the dramatic tensions of the plots that are much more than morality plays of good and evil, white hats and black hats.

NOTES

1. The title of the book is taken from the name of the desert in New Mexico, *jornada del muerto*.

2. Jeffrey Wolfe, *Ridin' West*, 1993.

3. Pierre Montet, *Everyday Life in Egypt in the Days of Rameses the Great*, trans. A. R. Maxwell-Hyslop and M.S. Drower (Westport, Conn., 1974), 319.

4. Ibid., 321.

5. Ibid., 328.

6. Hiroshi Obayashi, *Death and Afterlife* (Westport, Conn., 1992), 46.

7. T. W. Rolleston, *Myths and Legends of the Celtic Race* (New York, 1986), 131.

8. Louis L'Amour, *Hondo* (New York, 1953), 59.

9. Martin Benjamin, *Splitting the Difference* (Lawrence, Kans., 1990), 88.

10. Ibid.

11. see Harry Frankfurt, "The Importance of What We Care About" in *The Importance of What We Care About* (Cambridge, 1988), 80–94.

12. Ibid., 82–83.

13. Ibid., 83.

14. Ibid.

15. Ibid.

16. Ibid., 84.

17. Ibid., 85.

18. Benjamin, *Splitting the Difference*, 88.

19. Ludwig Wittgenstein, *On Certainiy* trans. D. Paul and G.E.M. Anscombe (Oxford, 1969), 29.

20. Benjamin, *Splitting the Difference*, 90.

21. Frankfurt, *The Importance of What We Care About*, 86.

22. Ibid.

23. Ibid.

24. Ibid., 87.

25. Robert Bolt, *A Man For All Seasons* (New York, 1962).

26. Throughout I will be using the term "easterner" as both a noun and an adjective. I do this, I hope, to avoid a confusion: by "easterner" I refer to a person from, or with the values of someone from, the eastern United States as represented in the films. When used as an adjective, as in "easterner values," I mean the values characteristic of an easterner, again as represented in the films.

27. Tompkins, *West of Everything*, 24.

· 2 ·

THE MOUNT AND THE MOUNTAINS

I

Clint Eastwood's *Pale Rider* opens with a terror raid by hired thugs of the mining baron, LaHood, on the homes and work site of a loosely organized group of independent miners. In the wake of the destruction, a teenage girl, Megan, buries her dog, a victim of the raid, and over the grave she recites the Twenty-third Psalm, interrupting each line to contradict the Biblical verses.

> "The Lord is my shepherd, I shall not want—
>   *But I do want!*
> He leadeth me beside still waters. He restoreth my soul—
>   *But they killed my dog!*
> Yea though I walk through the valley of the shadow of death,
>   I will fear no evil—
>   *But I am afraid!*
> For thou art with me. Thy rod and thy staff comfort me—
>   *We need a miracle!*
> Thy loving kindness and mercy shall follow me all the days of my life—
>   *If you exist!*
> And I shall dwell in the house of the Lord forever—
>   *But I'd like to get more of this life first!*"

She looks up to the snow-covered mountains and pleads for "Just one miracle." As she does, we see a rider emerging from the mountains on a pale horse. Megan shifts her Biblical references to the *Book of Revelation* and while reading, "and I saw, and behold, a pale horse, and its rider's name was Death," she sees the rider, known only as "the Preacher," come into view.

This is no ordinary minister of the gospel come to provide holy succor for the injuries of those in the mining camp. This is a gunslinger, a killer, who on some occasions, for reasons never revealed, reverses his collar. He is a preacher who never invokes the name of God. His only prayer is the ambiguous "For what we are about to receive may we be truly grateful." It is worth noting that he says this with a clearly this-worldly tone and expression while exchanging glances with both Megan and her mother.

The opening sequences of *Pale Rider* capture and convey the philosophical and cultural foundations of the ethics of the Western. That is, they vividly display what the Western, or at least the westerner, rejects and about what he (or it) cares or in what he is invested. In *Pale Rider*, as in most Westerns, the Judeo-Christian conceptions on which much of our traditional ethical understandings are based, are portrayed as impotent, useless, something belonging "back East," "an enormous cultural weight,"[1] a load that must be left behind if one is to survive and amount to anything on the frontier.

Tompkins argues that the Western positions itself as antithetical to Christianity. It does so, of course, because it invests the easterner with what a Christian cares about. Tompkins, I think correctly, places this rejection of Christianity in a literary/historical context: as emerging from a literary reaction to the Christian fiction of the late nineteenth century that was typically written for, and often by, women.[2] In fact, the way women are portrayed in Westerns, no doubt, owes much to the literary response of the first writers of Westerns to the domestic, female-oriented, Christian fiction of the period.

What books were the best-selling Christian fiction of the late nineteenth century? Tompkins points out that they were Harriet Beecher Stowe's *The Minister's Wooing*, Mrs. Humphry Ward's *Robert Ellesmere*, Charles Seldon's enormously popular *In His Steps*, Maria Cummins's *The Lamplighter*, and, of course, Lew Wallace's *Ben-Hur*. As Tompkins notes, only six years after the publication of Seldon's *In His Steps*, Owen Wister produced *The Virginian*. Not long after that Zane Grey wrote *Riders of the Purple Sage*. Though this may sound like it was nothing but a literary war, Tompkins reminds us that a nineteenth century women's movement was also emerging, threatening male mastery. She writes:

> The post-Civil War era saw a massive movement of women out of the home and into public life. Aptly termed 'social home-making,' the movement was inspired by women's participation in ante-bellum reform activities, which had been centered on church and home. 'We hear, 'A woman's place is at home,' wrote Carrie Nation, one of the great reformers of the post-Civil War years.' That is true, but what and where is home? Not the walls of a house. Not furniture, food or clothes. Home is where the heart is, where our loved ones are. If my son is in a drinking

place, my place is there. If my daughter, or the daughter of anyone else, my family or other family, is in trouble, my place is there. . . . Jesus said, 'Go out into the highways and hedges.' He said this to women, as well as men.'[3]

Nation's call was answered by thousands of women who took up all manner of social causes in the name of Christianity. A rising tide of civilizing and Christianizing not only was led by women, but threatened to wash away the very activities and beliefs that men held to be their special domain, what they cared most about. Women, some men must have feared, were taking over and, to make matters worse, they were doing so under the banner of Christian righteousness. To stand against that would require either a reformation of Christian dogma or a desertion of the religion altogether. After all, these women were out to convert the frontier and the wilderness, where a man could be a man, into the domain of the two institutions in which femininity dominated: the home and the church. Nation's home had no walls, and her church was founded on doctrines that threatened to emasculate the frontier spirit. A theological assault was, by and large, rejected, perhaps because those capable of taking on the task realized straightaway that the women did, in fact, have God (or at least scripture) on their side. Their speeches and writings positively dripped with supporting quotations from the Sermon on the Mount that were indisputably put to good and fair use. Desertion of the Christian ethic, at least in fiction if not in fact, and the construction of an alternative bastion to house an opposing world view, a radically different collection of cares, was apparently a more appealing endeavor. And in that bundle of cares both of those co-opted institutions, the home and the church, would have to be either rejected or excluded as unsuitable. In that philosophic and literary climate, the westerner that in the twentieth century would fill the silver screen was created. The writers of the frontier—Mark Twain, Owen Wister, Bret Harte, and Zane Grey—blazed that sagebrush trail for a century of Western film directors and script writers to ride, saddlebags packed with a world view that always is a rejection of, but much more than a rejection of, feminized Christianity.

Tompkins believes that the Western is really about the fear of men losing their position of dominance in society to women and "feminized Christianity."[4] It is a reinvention of a male myth. John Wayne, in a minor film, *Tall in the Saddle*, tells Gabby Hayes's character, "I don't feel sorry for anything that happens to a woman." My interest is not to dispute Tompkin's thesis. I want to concentrate on what the westerner (both hero and villain) in the films cares and does not care about and the ethics and metaethics that supervene on those cares and, of course, the world view that the films place in opposition to the cares of the westerner: the Christian feminine bundle of cares.

II

The anti-Christian stance in Westerns appears in a multitude of ways. For example, ordinary men (not the heroes or villains) are generally depicted as embued with Christian values, even living Christian lives. And it is they who are revealed to be incapable of rising to challenges, inadequate to the tasks crucial to surviving and flourishing in the West, in its towns and in its wide open spaces. They are fathers and husbands, storekeepers and farmers who are portrayed as constrained by ethical considerations that are inappropriate for the circumstances. They are emasculated and left defenseless by the civilized Christian ideals they have adopted or that have, more often than not, been forced on them by women. In *The Man Who Shot Liberty Valance*, a film I will discuss in more detail in chapter 6, we first meet Ransom Stoddard, played by James Stewart, as an easterner lawyer who is savagely beaten by the outlaw Liberty Valance. Valance rips up Stoddard's law books and says that what he is doing is giving the dude a lesson in Western law. Stoddard is portrayed as utterly incapable of effective response. In the early scenes of *Pale Rider* the shopkeeper, who is described as and seen to be a good Christian fellow, stands behind his window watching his friend, the independent miner Hull Barrett, being verbally insulted and mercilessly beaten. If the husbands and would-be husbands of the female leads remain in the story at all, in the *Shane*-type stories or ones with significant *Shane*-type elements, of which *Pale Rider, Will Penny, The Shootist, Hondo,* and *The Tall T* are examples, they may be able occasionally to display residual aggressive masculine traits when inspired by a true westerner, but, by and large, they are, in Tompkins's words, "enfeebled by the doctrines of feminized Christianity."[5] They are dominated by women.

In *Shane*, Marion decries the use of the gun to settle matters, and she opposes the shooting lesson Shane gives to her son, Little Joey. She wants a valley free of guns where families can be raised in peace and love. She will not accept Shane's explanation that a gun is just a tool like any other, only as good or as bad as the person who uses it. Perhaps she sees the gun as a phallic symbol, a powerful and deadly icon of the masculine. Perhaps that is what she wants banned from the valley.

In *Pale Rider*, Megan's mother, Sarah, pleads with her fiancé, Hull, to negotiate with the villain, and even the emasculated Hull recognizes that will be fruitless. Negotiation, mediation, arbitration are the civilized responses to conflict situations. In Westerns they are represented as feminine responses, and as utterly ineffectual.

In *Stagecoach*, the rule of women and their identification with both the Christian church and civilization itself is made manifestly clear when Dallas, the prostitute (with a heart of gold), is driven out of town by a gaggle of self-righteous females spouting Christian platitudes and marching to Christian hymns. *Stagecoach* also defines for us the two types of women who will appear in Westerns. There are the easterners, the crusaders for Christianity and its "civilized" family values, so many incarnations of Carrie Nation, and there are the prostitutes, virtually westerners, at least in attitude, though usually constrained by caring about some of the feminine easterner cares, especially those surrounding the concept of home, and so never fully westernized. It has always struck me as revealing, in some difficult-to-articulate way, that the good Christian easterner women of Westerns seem always to have and are referred to by full names, (or what Philip French[6] calls WASP-ish names) like Lucy Mallory (the cavalry officer's wife in *Stagecoach*), while the saloon women and the prostitutes bear the names of cities like Dallas (in *Stagecoach*), Chihuahua (in *My Darling Clementine*), and Vienna (in *Johnny Guitar*). I suppose Mrs. Miller (of *McCabe and Mrs. Miller*) is an exception, and perhaps her name was chosen for that very reason.

The prostitutes typically share more of the westerner's perspective than their Christian easterner sisters. For example, the prostitutes in *Unforgiven*, as a just penalty for the slashing of the face of one of their own, reject civilized ways of settling disputes and throw the town back into the violent days of vengeance. They will accept no form of restitution short of the death of the offenders. Most uncivilized! Most unChristian! And difficult for the recently civilized male population of the town, including the sheriff who is building a house, to understand. "Why would they want to go and do that?" he says.

Although male ministers make appearances (perhaps the most interesting is the ambiguous reverend in *The Searchers* who deftly doffs his clerical garb and leads the Texas Ranger unit, literally, at the drop of a collar), Christianity is almost always the province, domain, and retreat of women in Westerns. Bond Rogers, played by Lauren Bacall, in *The Shootist* is a good case in point. At first she vehemently expresses the desire to throw the notorious gunman J. B. Books, John Wayne's character, out of her boardinghouse. When she learns he is dying of cancer, she recants and begs his forgiveness for the most unChristian way she had acted. It is evident, to us and to her, that she bears the responsibilities of Christian service, even toward a most thoroughly nonChristian "assassin," as she calls him.

Christian rituals, services, and hymn singing in the films are typically organized by women or solely conducted by women and feeble, cowardly men. In *The Outlaw Josey Wales*, for example, only the women know the words and sing the hymn of thanksgiving, a hymn that, as it happens, is interrupted by more important matters, the appearance of a threat to life that calls the westerner into violent, and certainly not Christian, response. In *Will Penny*, Will (played by Charlton Heston) sheepishly admits to Catherine Allen and her son Horace that he does not know any Christmas carols. They are surprised and somewhat appalled. In *The Cowboys* the way for the young lads to become true cowboys, westerners, is for their mothers to give them up to the hardened training of a westerner, the obsessive Will Anderson (played by John Wayne), who rudely scrapes off their Christian, civilized veneer and turns them into calculating killers who risk death to avenge the savage murder of their surrogate father.

III

What are the central ethical doctrines and concepts of feminized Christianity? They are the familiar ones: turning the other cheek, loving (the *agape* variety) neighbors and enemies, antiviolence, leaving vengeance to God, the meek shall inherit the earth, showing mercy, being forgiving, humility, caring, kindness, doing onto others as one would have them do onto you. The admonitions of The Sermon on the Mount pretty well cover the territory occupied and defended by women in Westerns.

The Sermon on the Mount,[7] of course, derives its ethical force from divine command. The Jewish and Christian ethical traditions, unlike those of Greece and China, blur the distinction between moral and religious duties. In a Divine Command theory of ethics the sole ultimate standard of right and wrong is the will or law of God. So the Sermon is not just a listing of beatitudes, it is a series of commands from God, and it comes with divine rewards for obedience (the kingdom of heaven) and threats for disobedience. The Sermon also identifies the ethical authority of God not simply with God's divinity, but with the fact that God is good. The commands issue from a being that is not just superior to humans, but one that is morally superior to them as well.

Jesus orders the crowd on the Mount:

> You have heard that it was said, "You shall love your neighbor and hate your enemy." But I say to you, Love your enemies and pray for those who persecute you, so that you may be sons of your Father who is in

heaven; for he makes his sun rise on the evil and on the good, and sends rain on the just and on the unjust. For if you love those who love you, what reward have you? Do not even the tax collectors do the same? And if you salute only your brethren, what more are you doing than others? Do not even the Gentiles do the same? You, therefore, must be perfect, as your heavenly Father is perfect.[7]

That is certainly a tough order and one that runs against the grain of the westerner. It has also given Christian theologians difficulty when they try to understand it in the light of other aspects of their dogma. Some have ignored it completely. St. Augustine, for example, defends a position regarding the human condition that is decidedly not that implied by the perfection commandment. He wrote:

> God . . . created man good; but man, corrupt by choice and condemned by justice, has produced a progeny that is both corrupt and condemned . . . Thus, from a bad use of free choice, a sequence of misfortunes conducts the whole human race . . . from the original canker in its root to the devastation of a second and endless death.[8]

For Augustine, human history is the story of a continual degeneration, hardly a march to perfection.

> The race of mortal men has been a race condemned. Think first of that dreadful abyss of ignorance from which all error flows and so engulfs the sons of Adam in a darksome pool that no one can escape without the toll of toils and tears and fears."[9]

On the other side of the theological coin, however, were St. Irenaeus, who wrote during the second century, and Pelagius, a British monk in the fifth century. Irenaeus was concerned with trying to understand the significance of the expulsion from Paradise, the root of Augustine's original sin doctrine, in the light of the teachings of Christ on the Mount. He argued that the sin of Adam and Eve could not have been the forfeiture of perfection and any hope of its restoration by human actions. Instead, he maintained, that human beings must have been created in an imperfect state, but because human beings were created with free will, they are capable of self-improvement, of creating, by themselves, Godlike creatures, or what Irenaeus called "children of God." Irenaeus wrote: "Man was a child; and his mind was not yet fully mature; . . . How could he be trained in the good, without the knowledge of its contrary? . . . How then will any man be a God, if he has not first been made a man? How can any be perfect when he has only lately been made a man?"[10]

Pelagius argued that, on the Mount, Jesus orders human beings to perfect themselves. How, he wondered, can humans obey that holy command, if perfection is not within their power? If God commanded it, it must be possible for the human race to perfect itself, to progress to better and better states until Heaven on Earth is achieved. If perfection is not possible because of something in human nature that blocks it, God would be a sadistic divinity, ordering humans to do what they cannot help but fail to do. The optimism of the Christian women in Westerns is no doubt Pelagian. They seem convinced that humans working together can perfect their social relationships and that the wilderness is just the place to build the second Garden of Eden, a social utopia. The westerner gives the impression that he does not so much care if the women make the attempt and even succeed in creating some version of Heaven on Earth, perhaps a City of God, with equal emphasis on "city" and "God." He only wants them to try to do it somewhere else, somewhere East, and some other time. Of course, he is typically ready to expose sham attempts to do so, attempts that try to disguise other, less Christian, motives. In *High Plains Drifter*, for example, the townspeople, or at least their leaders, may be determined to build a little heaven of a town, but the westerner is fully prepared to expose its underlying corruptions, paint it red, and turn it into Hell.

Arguably the most revolutionary plank in Jesus's ethical platform on the Mount was his requiring that his followers forgive those who do them injury. It should be clear to anyone even vaguely acquainted with the books of Exodus and Deuteronomy and other ancient legal texts, that forgiveness, if it is even hinted at, is reserved for God's discretion. The Mosaic law expressly adopts the talion formula (*lex talionus*) of other ancient codes: an eye for an eye, a tooth for a tooth, a life for a life. God was thought to be the only entity with the power and authority to forgive. Jesus, however, has his followers pray: "And forgive us our trespasses, as we also have forgiven those who trespass against us," and he comments, "For if you forgive men their trespasses, your heavenly Father also will forgive you; but if you do not forgive men their trespasses, neither will your Father forgive your trespasses."[11] It seems clear that Jesus is maintaining that God's forgiveness is earned by human forgiveness. In fact, it seems to depend on it, to be triggered by it. Only if you forgive others the wrongs done by them to you, do you get forgiveness from God. But what is it to forgive?

Human forgiveness, Bishop Joseph Butler tells us, is related to the forswearing of resentment,[12] the resolute overcoming of the sort of anger and hatred that we quite naturally direct toward someone who has unjustifiably harmed us. But resentment is the passion that defends one's self-respect against those who violate one's person. Little wonder that the westerner cannot understand the easterner Christian's call for forgiving of enemies. A person who does not resent moral injuries done to him or her lacks self-respect, and if anything is important to both the hero and the villain of the Western, it is self-respect. The classic repartee before the climactic gunfight is filled, on both sides, with assaults on dignity and respect. Watch the duel in Grafton's saloon between Shane and Wilson:

> Wilson: I wouldn't push too far, if I were you . . .
> Shane: So, you're Jack Wilson.
> Wilson: What's that to you, Shane?
> Shane: I've heard about you.
> Wilson: What have you heard, Shane?
> Shane: I've heard that you're a lowdown Yankee liar.
> Wilson: Prove it.

The call to forgive is the call to forswear resentment, and that is the call to relinquish one's self-respect.

The westerner would prefer to remain both unforgiven and unforgiving, rather than to accede to the Christian's code, rather than to forswear resentment against those who have offended his person. What, after all, is the value of residence in the Kingdom of Heaven, if the cost is one's self-respect? The rejection of forgiveness, both given and taken, is a defining characteristic of the westerner. He is usually portrayed as having little else than self-respect. He typically rides in out of the mountains with just his saddle bags and a blanket roll. He is generally not a man of property, and, if he once had a position in a community back East, he has long since abandoned it and cannot return to it. Shane makes that point in many ways, not the least of which is with his clothing. His ill-fated attempt to settle down and work with the homesteaders is marked by his doffing his well-worn buckskins. He buys and wears the clothing of a farmer. But when he realizes that he cannot fit into the homesteader community, that only he is a match for the hired gun of the cattle baron Rikers, and that he must ride back into the mountains, into the West, he again dresses in the buckskins.

Jeffrie Murphy writes: "The primary value defended by the passion of resentment is self-respect, . . . proper self-respect is essentially tied to the passion of resentment, and . . . a person who does not resent moral injuries done to him . . . is almost necessarily a person lacking in self-respect."[13] Peter Strawson elaborates that if we do not resent occasions when our rights are violated, all we show is that we do not take them very seriously, or that we do not think we have them at all.[14] As Murphy notes, "Forgiveness may indeed restore relationships, but to seek restoration at all cost—even at the cost of one's very human dignity—can hardly be a virtue."[15]

In literally hundreds of Westerns, the female lead begs the hero, or another lesser male character, to forswear resentment for an injury that has been done to him. We see it in *Shane* and *Pale Rider* and in *The Outlaw Josey Wales*, but nowhere is it clearer in all of the respects of the clash of cares between the westerner and the easterner, the male and the Christian female, than in *The Searchers*. Ethan Edwards, John Wayne's character, has organized the men of the community to avenge the brutal deaths of the woman he loved and her husband, his brother. Mrs. Jorgensen pleads with Ethan not to turn her boy into a creature of vengeance. Ethan doesn't answer her. Instead, he gives her a brief look that bespeaks volumes. The look says, "Have you no self-respect? Do you want your son to grow up without self-respect?" The suggestion, from the point of view of the westerner, is that resentment is a good thing because of its direct link to the sustaining of self-respect and dignity, which are taken to be self-evidently good things. That point can be made with just a brief stare.

The cost of forgiveness well may be dignity. When looked at in this way, something of the enormity of what Jesus requires and what Marion (in *Shane*), Sarah (in *Pale Rider*), and Mrs. Jorgensen (in *The Searchers*) are asking for may be understood. The westerner seldom deigns to verbalize his response.

Murphy does defend the position that forgiveness is acceptable in those cases where it is consistent with maintaining self-respect, respect for others as full-fledged moral agents, and when it does not amount to complicity in, acquiescence to, or condoning of the injury that has been suffered.[16] Such cases are going to be rare, and so on this account, forgiveness as a general rule would seem to have remarkably little moral value. The sacrifice of dignity and self-respect is too high a price, or at least that is what a westerner would conclude.

Jean Hampton responds to Murphy by defending the Christian account of forgiveness. She maintains that forgiveness is the way to restore the harm-causer to a relationship with the injured party. She writes, "Consider the Hebrew words used in the Old Testament to refer to forgiveness. The words *kipper* meaning 'to cover,' *nasa* meaning 'to lift up, or carry away,' and *salach* probably meaning 'to let go' are all used to describe forgiveness; and they are each, in different ways, metaphors for the forgiver's removal of sin from the wrongdoer. Forgiveness is understood as 'covering the sin so that each party can approach the other without the sin in full view.'"[17] In effect, the person who has been wronged, harmed, she tells us, forgets, in a nonliteral sense, the injury. The harm that was caused, then, supposedly, is not viewed; it is covered, as a hindrance, an interference, to the continuing relationship between the two parties, the harm-doer and the harmed. A civil relationship between the two becomes possible or possible again.

Hampton's account of forgiveness makes evident why the concept is so important to the easterners in the films (especially the women, excepting the prostitutes of *Unforgiven*). Forgiveness, understood in the way recommended by Hampton, is an essential building block of civilized, urbanized life. It is a requirement, it would seem, of community; and community is what the easterners in the films decidedly care about. They want places where they can bring up children. They want schools, churches, paved streets, electric streetcars, security, the whole civilized works. Mrs. Jorgensen (in *The Searchers*) expresses the feminine sentiment. Someday, she says, this country is going to be a fine place, even if it needs her and her family's bones in the ground before that day dawns. She is a true pioneer. She is in the West to transform it into a home, a community, and she is prepared to sacrifice by forgiving injuries done to her, even the killing of her only son, to bring about a civil state. The women in the Western are, by and large, what in recent parlance would be called, communitarians. For them, the desert must be turned into vegetable and flower gardens. The mud and the dirt must be paved, communities created and sustained where once there was wilderness.

One of the things, perhaps not a minor one, that makes *Unforgiven* so fascinating a film is the fact that the role played by the Christian women in most of the other Westerns is taken on in *Unforgiven* by the townsmen, led by their sheriff. They are the ones who insist that the sin be "covered" so that they can get on with civilizing their town and themselves. The prostitutes refuse to surrender their dignity to the community. Little Bill, the sheriff who reverts to ultraviolent methods to control the influx of gunfighters to his town, actually no longer sees himself as a westerner. He's building a house. He was once a famous gunslinging lawman, but he has "gone civilized" and has even adopted a code of justice in the case of the scarred prostitute, a code that might pass muster in many contemporary jurisdictions. The uncompromising, vengeful whores, however, have produced a situation that, seemingly quite against his will, drives him back to his barbarous ways. But then, the building of the house is not going all that well.

The notion of forgetting that Hampton reads as crucial to forgiveness is, however, problematic. What is it to "nonliterally" forget? I confess that I am mostly in the dark. Hampton certainly takes great pains to make clear that forgiving in her "nonliteral" forgetting sense is not condoning the wrongdoing. It also is not ignoring the offense or having some sort of short-term memory loss with respect to it. It is not a matter of waiting for the harm-causer or wrongdoer to get around to proving that he or she has changed his or her evil ways. If that were the case, then it would not so much be forgiveness as it would be disassociating the person from the deed on the basis of the belief that the person has changed and so is not the same person who committed the injurious deed. No such metamorphosis in the offender is required for forgiveness. In fact, if a radical personality change did occur, there might be no need for forgiving. What sense does it make to forgive someone for doing something that you no longer regard as one of his or her actions? So, it is both forgetting and not forgetting. One remembers the act, but forgets that the person who performed the act, something one also does not forget, performed the act. Simply, one does not let the fact that the person performed the act destroy one's relationship to the person.

Unprovoked forgetting seems to be an essential part of the forgiving package on Hampton's account. No matter what happens in the mind or behavior of the injurer, forgiveness is not guaranteed. It depends solely on the injured party's decisions and subsequent behavior. A number of people serving serious time in our prisons have claimed to have undergone moral transformations; but that fact, if it is a fact, does not create for those they have wronged an obligation to forgive them. Forgiveness-as-forgetting is a gratuitous act or stance made or taken by the injured party. Of course, when we take into consideration that Jesus on the Mount makes forgiving a condition for divine forgiveness, the gratuitousness of the act might be doubted.

Forgiveness, as Hampton explicates the notion, involves no small amount of trust. That is, the injured party, when forgiving, is committed to trusting that the wrongdoer, despite the way he or she has acted and the bad character traits he or she has exhibited, still is "good enough" for continued association. In effect, the act of forgiveness entails, on Hampton's account, the conception of persons as more than the sum of their actions and their character traits, a basic view the westerner outright rejects. Hampton's way of putting this is "Forgiveness is precisely the decision that *he* isn't bad."[18] To be able to forgive someone, you must believe that underneath the actions and the display of immoral character, he or she is really not as Hampton puts it "a morally rotten individual." In other words, forgiveness entails a conception of the underlying nature of humans as inherently or basically good, or at least not bad. People, at least with respect to their moral worth, are not to be identified with their deeds. Though their actions are bad, they may not be. This idea is, of course, a primary tenet of what John Kekes calls "choice morality,"[19] and it is an essential component of the popular view, held by Kant, that moral worth and moral merit can and should be disassociated. The westerner does not, however, disassociate worth and merit, persons and their actions. The fact that Joey Garza, one of the villains of *Streets of Laredo*, acts in vicious, murderous, evil ways, is proof positive that Joey Garza is wicked and deserving of no forgiveness, a lesson his mother Maria learns only when he kills her.

When it comes to the measure of a person, the westerner is interested in nothing more than what he or she has done, a basic precept of what Kekes calls "character morality." Hence, the Ringo Kid is drawn to Dallas, the outcast prostitute, because of the kindly way she acts at the stage way station and certainly not because he holds a view about the underlying good of all people. Throughout all of the Westerns, persons are understood by westerners to be what they have done, nothing more, nothing less. Reputations based on deeds are the identity of the person and determine the amount of respect one is shown. In *McCabe and Mrs. Miller*, McCabe, a gambler with a reputation for having killed a famous outlaw with a derringer, wants to become an entrepreneur in the gambling and prostitution business, but it is his reputation as a killer that garners him respect among the townsfolk. In *Unforgiven*, William Munny's reputation as a brutal killer of anything that walks or crawls marks him. But those are just two of what could become a volume of nothing but examples.

It is worth noting, as Hampton does, that forgiveness should not be confused with mercy. To be merciful is to treat a person less harshly than he or she deserves or than one has a right to treat him or her, given the moral trespass committed by that person. Westerners can be merciful. In fact, it often pleases them to extend mercy by not, for example, killing someone who has injured them. In *The Ballad of Cable Hogue*, for example, Cable was left to die in the desert by his two unscrupulous partners, Taggart and Bowen. After he becomes a success by finding water where everyone said there was no water, the two reappear. Although he is forced to kill Taggart, he extends mercy to Bowen and, even, in the end, bequeaths him the waterhole and the lucrative business he has built around it. By rights, the westerner might say, he could have killed them both on sight, and he had planned to do so. But when Bowen seems to Cable no longer worth killing and more pathetic than anything else, Cable shows pity and even compassion. The westerner might hit the person who has offended him and/or humiliate him in some way. Bowen is forced to strip to his long johns to teach him a lesson, but the full and just penalty will not be exacted.

Typically, however, the hero shows mercy only to some lesser villain or accomplice, and usually the hero includes a warning to the offender that is supposed to be carried back to the real villain as a part of the mitigated punishment. In any event, there need not be any expression of forgiveness in the merciful act. Cable does not forgive or forget, but he is merciful.

Another point about forgiving: forgiving is not excusing. As J. L. Austin in his seminal work on excuses makes clear, to excuse is to admit that the thing that was done "wasn't a good thing to have done, but to argue that it is not quite fair or correct to say baldly 'X (the offender) did A (the offending act).' "[20] To excuse is to admit that the act was bad, but that the actor was not, or not fully, responsible for doing it. Consequently, excuses are only in order when certain conditions effecting the offender's actions can rightly be said to have occurred: it was partly accidental, unintentional, under duress, incidental to what he was really doing, or something along those lines. If someone has a good excuse, they seldom are in need of forgiveness. Jesus on the Mount does not have his followers pray, "Excuse us as we excuse others for what they do to us."

The westerner not only does not forgive, but seldom accepts excuses. John Wayne's persona in a number of films, and especially in *Red River* and *The Cowboys* makes this abundantly clear. His Captain Bligh-like demeanor as Tom Dunson in *Red River* includes an unwillingness to allow any excuses for foul-ups on the trail. When a cowhand accidentally starts a stampede by rattling pots and pans, Dunson will neither forgive nor accept excuses. In *The Cowboys*, Wayne goes after a boy, a stutterer, who did not call for help when another of the young boys on the cattle drive was drowning in a river crossing. The dialogue goes as follows:

Anderson (John Wayne): You almost got him killed. You know that?
Stutterer: But I tried to tell you.
Anderson: The Hell you did.
Stutterer: I tried hard.
Anderson: If you'd have been out in that water, we'd a heard you loud and clear.
Stutterer: I couldn't get the words out.
Anderson: You could've if you'd have wanted to. You just didn't want to bad enough.
Stutterer: Before God, I tried.
Anderson: Trying don't get it done. Fact is, you almost let your friend choke to death out in that river.
Stutterer: I'd rather have died than done that.
Anderson: Then you're a liar.
Stutterer: It ain't my fault I stutter.

Anderson: Listen to me, you whining little whelp. You're going to stop that stuttering or get the hell out of here. You're going to stop it or go home. Do you hear me?

Stutterer (whispered): Son of a bitch.

Anderson: What did you say?

Stutterer (loudly): You goddamn son of a bitch.

Anderson: Say that again.

Stutterer: You goddamn, mean son of a bitch.

Anderson: Say it faster.

Stutterer: You goddamn, mean, dirty son of a bitch.

Anderson (satisfied): I wouldn't make a habit of calling me that, son.

IV

The Sermon on the Mount also includes the statement of the Christian Golden Rule. The Revised Standard translation is "So whatever you wish that men would do to you, do so to them." (Confucius seems to have formulated a similar rule about five hundred years before the Sermon.) In the comedy Western *Waterhole #3*, the ballad running throughout the film repeats, "It's the code of the West, to your own self be true. It's the code of the West to do unto others, do unto others, before they can do it to you." So much for the Golden Rule in the westerner's collection of cares? Not exactly. What makes the song (and the film) comic is the twisting of the westerner's perspective, or, at least, the heroic westerner's perspective. The code of the West, as depicted in the films, is not to do onto others before they can do it to you. J. B. Books (John Wayne), in *The Shootist*, explains his code to Gillom Rogers, the son of the woman who runs the boardinghouse, in the following conversation:

Gillom: Mr. Books.

Books: Yeah.

Gillom: How'd you ever kill so many men?

Books: I lived most of my life in the wild country and you set a code of laws to live by.

Gillom: What laws?

Books: I won't be wronged, I won't be insulted, and I won't be laid a hand on. I don't do these things to other people, and I require the same from them.

Gillom: How could you get into so many fights and then always come out on top? I nearly tied you shooting.

Books: Friend, there was nobody up there shootin' back at you. It isn't always being fast or even accurate that counts. It's being willing. Now,

> I found out early that most men regardless of cause or need aren't willing. They blink an eye or draw a breath before they pull a trigger. I won't.

"I won't be wronged, insulted, or have a hand laid on me and I don't do those things to others" sounds not unlike a specification of "Do unto others as you would have them do unto you." Of course, a great deal may fall under the first category, and what the westerner regards as a wrong may not be in agreement with what the easterner thinks is a wrong. The matter of insult and laying a hand on one's physical person work to define the integrity of the westerner's personal space and reputation. An invasion of personal space is not countenanced, nor is an act of slander. In large measure, this may be because, as noted earlier, the westerner seldom has any property other than what he carries in his saddlebags. All he is, is his physical person and his reputation, and he can be injured in very few ways other than by direct assaults on his personal space and his name. He reciprocally grants only such a limited number of personal protections to others. He won't lay a hand on you and he won't defame your name, unless, of course, you have deserved it because of the way you have violated him.

The westerner is not an avenging angel. He is not in the business of righting wrongs wherever he rides across them. He is not the cowboy equivalent of the Caped Crusader. The wrongs must always relate to some harm suffered either by him directly or by someone with whom he has established a relationship, even an affectionate relationship. Hence, Shane does not ride into the Teton Valley in order to drive out the Rikers. He is looking for work and associates himself with the Starretts and suffers personal affronts for doing so. The Preacher (in *Pale Rider*) not only comes to the aid of the independent miners, he has an old personal score to settle with the gunmen hired by the mining baron. Ethan Edwards's search is provoked because of his deep affection for his brother's wife Martha, as well as other family ties. The Clint Eastwood character in *High Plains Drifter* punishes the townspeople of Lago and kills the outlaws, we come to learn, because he is the reincarnation of the local sheriff who the townsfolk watched being whipped to death by those very outlaws. William Munny's assault on the men in the saloon in *Unforgiven* is provoked by the sheriff's vicious killing of his friend Ned. In fact, even the terrible beating Munny himself received from the sheriff was not enough to motivate him to attack the town. In short, the westerner does not just butt into a bad situation, make it right, then ride off into the sunset. On the whole, he is remarkably tolerant.

It is generally believed that the Golden Rule presupposes a uniformity of human nature—a uniformity of tastes, interests, needs, desires, etc. Such an assumption would give sense to Bertrand Russell's quip against the Rule: "There's no accounting for taste." Kant offered a rather different set of criticisms. The Golden Rule is not applicable, he maintained, to cases that involve only one person, such as suicide. The suicide only treats himself or herself; he or she does not treat others in ways he or she would not want the others to treat him or her. So suicide, under the Golden Rule should be morally permissible. Still, Kant and many other moral theorists argue that suicide is morally forbidden. In Westerns, suicide, when it is portrayed at all, which is rare, is shown to be the escape of the weak or the defeated. Two examples come to mind. One is in the ersatz Western *Dances with Wolves*, when the commander of a fort commits suicide after giving the lead character his assignment to a more desolate location. The other is in *Streets of Laredo* where a sheriff who has been humiliated, severely beaten, and locked in his own jail by Captain Woodrow Call is reported to have committed suicide.

Another type of case, also noted by Kant, seems to evade the Golden Rule on the usual interpretations and is more closely associated with the westerner's point of view. The Golden Rule seems to have nothing to say against a fully self-sufficient person, one who wants no aid from others, refraining from being kind or benevolent to others. He neither expects nor wants benevolence or help from others and he sees no reason to extend it to them. Many of the characters portrayed by Clint Eastwood in his "Man with No Name" series (both those directed by Sergio Leone and those directed by Eastwood) seem to be of this sort. For example, in *High Plains Drifter* the drifter, when asked by the hotel owner's wife, whom he has just bedded, why he came to the town of Lago, says "I was just stopping by for a bottle of whiskey and a nice hot bath." "Mister," she responds, "whatever you say is fine with me. But you'd better be careful. You're the kind of person who makes people afraid." He smirks, "It's what people know about themselves inside that makes them afraid." He dresses and goes out to continue to humiliate and insult the townspeople, and, in the process, literally to turn Lago into Hell. Despite training the townsfolk to protect themselves, he knows full well that he will want and get no real help from them when the killers return. He, and he alone, will ultimately have to confront them. He exudes the confidence of self-sufficiency that makes clear that he feels he has no reason to extend any kindness or consideration to the pathetic, frightened townsfolk. He wants and expects nothing for himself from them.

These types of behavior will evade the Golden Rule only if the rule is interpreted in a particular fashion: that whatever in particular one would want done to oneself, one should do to others. An alternative general interpretation, however, is available: One has to consider not what in particular one would have others do to or for oneself, but rather the general ways in which one would have others act in their treatment of oneself. Abstract your general wishes from your particular desires. You would probably want people to take account of your interests, needs, and desires even though yours might be very different from theirs and either satisfy them or not willfully frustrate them. So on this account, the Golden Rule requires a person to take into consideration the wishes, desires, etc., of others and accord them the respect and consideration he or she would want them to accord to his or her wishes, desires, etc. What the Golden Rule seems to require, on this account, is that we treat others in accordance with the same principles and standards we would have others apply to their treatment of us. So the Golden Rule is compatible with differences in interests, tastes, desires, wishes, etc. and does not presuppose a uniformity of human beings.

Books's version of the rule seems entirely compatible with this reading, so the westerner might be said to share, at least in this regard, an important tenet with the Christianized easterner and especially the women in the films. Of course, the problem is that the westerner and the easterner may utterly disagree on the principles and standards by which they want to be treated.

V

The Christian ethical doctrines, when rationalized and formalized, provide the foundations for ethics for theorists from Kant to contemporary feminists. When the prohibitions of the Ten Commandments are added to the mix, a fuller picture emerges of what, by and large, the westerner in the films rejects with respect to ethics and ethical theory. The prohibition against stealing, especially another's livestock, survives in the westerner's ethics, but it is justified on decidedly nonChristian, perhaps no more than pragmatic, grounds. Lying, most emphatically, is not countenanced. In *The Cowboys*, Will Anderson rejects Amos Watts (played by Bruce Dern), a job seeker for the cattle drive. The confrontation goes as follows:

> Anderson: How long were you with Fance?
> Amos Watts: Well, sir, the last eight years. What a lovely old man he is. I
>   tell you, if we weren't three of the damnedest fools, we'd be there
>   with him right now.

Anderson: And if you were, you'd be in a pine box. I was a pallbearer at his funeral, five years ago.

Amos Watts: Well, I've been caught at it, haven't I? Mister Anderson, I'm sorry I lied to you. I got them names out of the stockman's brand book. You see, we're fresh outta jail, and you tell that to people and they just turn a deaf ear on you.

Anderson: Well, I'm afraid I can't use you.

Amos Watts: How do you mean you can't use us?

Anderson: I won't use you.

Amos Watts: You mean that you're going to be like everyone else and not give us a chance to redeem ourselves?

Anderson: I don't hold jail against you, but I hate a liar.

Amos Watts: Well, you're a hard man, Mr. Anderson.

Anderson: Well, it's a hard life. I got work to do.

We learn later in the film that Amos Watts and his gang are sadistic murdering outlaws, but Anderson never asks him why they were in jail. They were probably incarcerated for some heinous crime or other, but the crime and the jailtime are nothing to Anderson next to the fact of the lie. We might, of course, conjecture about whether Anderson would have asked Watts about the reason for his having been in jail had he not caught him in a bold-faced lie, and whether he would have held some crimes rather than others against Watts.

In *Will Penny*, the vicious Preacher Quint reminds us that "The Lord don't side with them that lies." Even the villain will not abide a liar. In *Hondo*, the westerner is asked: "You think truth is the most important thing?" And he responds, "The measure of a man."

Philosopher Michael Awalt showed me a silent Tom Mix film in which the hero is described on one of the caption screens in the following way: "He asks no questions and gives no answers." Those who display a facility for language are suspect. Lying is, after all, an art of language. The language of the true westerner is clipped, minimalistic. The liar, however, is but one of the language users the westerner despises. Politicians, salesmen, newspaper reporters, all of those whose businesses involve extensive language-using are treated with contempt. In *The Tall T* the effeminate male is referred to in the following way: "He's a talker . . . Ain't he something." Westerners seem to regard only their "desperate shorthand" (Tompkins's term) as meaningful speech acts. All other language-using is contrasted with acting or really doing something and is assigned to easterners in the films. "Language is gratuitous at best; at worst it is deceptive. It takes the place of things, screens them from view, creates a shadow world where anything can be made to look like anything else."[21]

In the Western, language is the province and the last resort of women, even more than it is that of cowardly and dishonorable men. Women do a lion's share of the talking in westerns. The director of a series of Randolph Scott films in the fifties, Budd Boetticher bold-facedly stated, "What counts is what the heroine provokes, or rather what she represents . . . In herself the woman has not the slightest importance."[22] What she represents are the virtues of conversation, discussion, compromise. Women seem always to be telling the hero and the other men that solutions to their problems are to be had by talking things out. The hero, typically in mumbled half-sentences, politely disagrees. But still she goes on, and finally when events are about to reach their climax, she continues to jabber. Tess Millay, in *Red River*, greets Matt Garth in the hotel in Abilene with the following:

> Tess: He's camped two or three miles outside of town. He says he'll be here just after sunup. He says he's going to kill you. What's the matter? Is something . . . ? Oh, I must look like I'm in mourning. I didn't mean it that way or I wouldn't . . . No, Matthew, no. I know you've only a few hours, but listen for just a minute, that's all, then I won't talk about it anymore. Just a minute. He hasn't changed his mind, Matthew. He's like something you can't move . . . I was going to ask you to run, but no, I'm not. You're too much like him. Oh stop me, Matthew. Stop me . . . God bless you, Matthew.

And in *Shane*, Marion is reduced to pathetic whining and pleading with Joe not to take on the Rikers and Wilson.

> Marion: It's just pride, a silly kind of pride. Don't I mean anything to you Joe? Doesn't Joey? . . . Don't let him go, Shane. Don't anyone go . . . This isn't worth a life, anybody's life. What are you fighting for? This shack? This little piece of ground? And nothing but work, work, work? I'm sick of it. I'm sick of trouble. Joe, let's move, let's go on . . . There must be some way. Shane, some way? (screams).

As Tompkins notes, "When the crunch comes, women shatter into words."[23] Westerners act.

In *Will Penny*, Catherine pleads with Will to give up his cowboying ways, marry her, and take up farming. She responds to his concern that she is already married, by telling him that there was never any love between her and her husband. She has fallen in love with Will. All of her arguments and pleas fall on deaf ears. Will cannot see himself changing a lifetime of being a cowboy to take up a plow, and he cannot overcome his moral concern that she is married. To her credit, Catherine, like Tess, finally realizes that she is not going to change Will's mind with words, and she shuts up.

V

Christian doctrines, practices, and rituals are primary sources of humor in Westerns. They are ridiculed in word, song, and action. In *The Cowboys* we are told, "There ain't no Sundays west of Omaha." In *The Quick and the Dead* (1987) the following dialogue occurs between an easterner, Mac-Askill, and the westerner, Conn Vallian (played by Sam Elliott):

> MacAskill: I'm one of those fools because I listened to you. So now, instead of our horses, these men want our blood.
> Vallian: Let me tell you something, MacAskill. You've been acting like the meek are going to inherit the earth. The meek ain't goin' to inherit nothin' west of Chicago.

In *The Plainsman*, Gary Cooper, playing Wild Bill Hickock, tells an easterner woman, "There ain't no Sundays west of Kansas City, no law west of Hays City, and no God west of Carson City." In the musical *Paint Your Wagon*, Ben Rumson (played by Lee Marvin) provides the creed of the westerner when he responds to his partner's (played by Clint Eastwood) concern that a woman can't have two husbands. Rumson tells him:

> Rumson: Out here we make up our rules as we go along. This ain't Michigan. It's gold country. Why Hell, it's the golden country, untouched and uncontaminated by human hands. It's where people can someday look civilization straight in the eye and spit. And you don't have to please anybody. And you don't have to love thy neighbor. You leave the bastard alone. It's wild, human, and free. And all over this nation they preach against it every Sunday.

Wild, human, and free! And being driven to death by the relentless surge of easterner civilized Christianity.

VI

Alasdair MacIntyre points out that the ethics of Christianity, derived from the ethics preached in the Sermon on the Mount and in the Pauline letters, caused the Christians a paradox when applied to society at large and as guideposts for the behavior of people over an indefinite period of time.[24] It was an ethics originally "addressed to individuals or small communities to separate themselves off from the rest of society."[25] It was an ethics intended to cover what the early Christians believed would be a rather short time between the present and the coming of the Kingdom of God. It was not intended for a pluralistic society that might continue on indefinitely. In effect, Christian ethics are based on both a deep-seated belief in the imminent Second Coming and a bold-faced appeal to self-love. For example, Jesus tells his followers to "love thy neighbor as *thyself*." And in virtually every verse of the Sermon on the Mount we find the prudential appeal: a promised reward in the kingdom of heaven. The implication also is that that Kingdom is temporally "just around the corner," that the present generation will welcome its arrival.

The Kingdom, of course, did not come, has not come, and most Christians, not counting those who make the covers of supermarket tabloids, are loath to assign any specific date to its arrival. So how are Christian ethics to be applied to ordinary human life in a noninterim society? MacIntyre writes: "It is not surprising that insofar as Christianity has propounded moral beliefs and elaborated moral concepts for ordinary human life, it has been content to accept contextual frameworks from elsewhere."[26]

MacIntyre provides three examples of frameworks that Christian ethics has accepted and incorporated in its cause over the centuries. Although MacIntyre places them correctly in historical context, all three, as well as their messianic forefather, have survived into this century. The first is the hierarchical social structure of the medieval feudal community. Using that framework, Christian ethics borrows the notions of hierarchy and role and can be interpreted as predominantly communitarian. On this account, the community, understood in terms of a structural hierarchy of well-defined stations and roles for all members, constitutes the realm of the moral life. In such a framework, a person is defined, and defines himself or herself, in terms of his or her place in the communal system. The ethical commands of God are understood to be not unlike the commands of a feudal lord to his tenants. They are to be obeyed because of their source. They emanate from a being who is both all-powerful and good. It is no wonder that humility becomes a virtue in this Christian ethical scheme.

The well-organized and well-run community, on the feudal framework, is the gauge of success of the implementation of the values of Christian ethics. The Christian God is the terribly huge Lord of all, whose commands to be meek and peace-loving and merciful, etc. are to be obeyed, not only because obedience guarantees personal salvation, but because it is also good for the community. The concept of vocation dominates the social thinking of the feudal Christian, and it can identify its roots in Paul's first letter to the Corinthians. In effect, vocation meant that every member of the community had a function to fulfill and those functions were, themselves, the product of the divine ordering of human life, which, of course, by its nature would be good. "What mattered was . . . the office which that individual occupied. The office itself is capable of precise measurement, capable of a purely objective assessment: it is to be measured by its own contents . . . [T]he office and the power it contained were not of human origin or making but of allegedly divine provenance."[27]

The art of the medieval period, the illuminations in manuscripts and the great church paintings that size humans not as they actually looked but according to their social, and therefore religious, rank, provides a visual reference for the borrowed feudal conceptual framework for the ethics. Bishops and cardinals were huge, the serfs tiny.[28] The feudal framework for Christian ethics seemed, then, to place a much higher regard on the integrity of social structure than on the individual human. The shift to the latter emphasis would come with Luther and the nontheological political theories that followed in his train. It constitutes the second framework adopted for Christian ethics, as noted by MacIntyre.

The second framework elevates the individual to the central place in the moral life. The social structure no longer dominates; in fact, it is viewed as but a product of the freely made contracts of individual people. The Christian moral life is not lived in and through the community and its stations. MacIntyre notes that three main concepts emerged from this Lutheran perspective on Christian ethics: (1) moral rules, though they are unconditional in their demands on individuals, lack rational justification; (2) people are sovereign in their choices; and (3) the secular world has its own justifications and norms that are independent of moral law and the moral life.[29] The moral life is an individual internal matter. Or, it is a matter between an individual and God, who could, of course, access the inner life of the individual. Morally, "the events that matter all occur in the psychological transformation of the faithful individual."[30]

Given such a framework, Luther's advocacy of the massacre of the peasants becomes more comprehensible. Secular business is outside of the ethical realm. In the best tradition of Jesus' teaching, one is to render unto Caesar what is Caesar's and unto God what is God's. The secular administration of the German princes was threatened by the peasants' revolt, and if the efficient and effective way to handle the revolt was to massacre the peasants, then that is what one should expect of secular authority. Luther, apparently, had no ethical qualms about that, because, for him, it lay outside the ethical realm. As MacIntyre notes, "the author who is the Luther of secular power is Machiavelli."[31]

The truly radical element of the Lutheran framework was, of course, its individualism and the equality of all individuals in the moral realm. The ethical relationship of people to each other, under this framework, as compared to that of the feudal Christian, was contractual rather than a matter of status. That idea, born in Luther, would become the central piece in the political theories of Hobbes and Locke, who would also recognize, from Machiavelli, the centrality of the concern for the control of power in a social life of freely contracting individuals where God no longer dominates the sociopolitical scene.

But who or what is this Lutheran individual Christian? MacIntyre notes, "When Luther wants to explain what an individual is, he does so by pointing out that when you die, it is you who die, and no one else can do this for you. It is as such, stripped of all social attributes, abstracted, as a dying man is abstracted, from all his social relations, that the individual is continually before God."[32] I am reminded of the lines from Kipling's poem:

> Stand up, stand up now, Tomlinson,
> And answer loud and high
> The good that ye did for the sake of men
> Or ever ye came to die—. . .
> Oh I have a friend on earth, he said,
> That was my priest and guide,
> And well would he answer all for me
> If he were at my side.—
> For that ye strove in neighbor-love,
> It shall be written fair,
> But now ye wait at Heaven's Gate
> And not in Berkeley Square:
> Though we called your friend from his bed
> this night,
> He could not speak for you,
> For the race is run by one and one and
> Never by two and two.[33]

It is worth noting that such a description is not far from the one John Rawls provides of the people in the Original Position, except, of course, that Luther (and Kipling) endow this stripped individual with the contingent choices of action he or she has made through life. Rawls's people are even more abstracted. They are almost pure rational decision makers. F. H. Bradley assaulted this sort of Lutheranism in "My Station and Its Duties." For him, of course, it had become Kantianism. He argued that a person stripped of his or her social ties did not and could not exist. Bradley wrote, "He is what he is because he is a born and educated social being, and a member of an individual social organism; . . . if you make abstraction of all this, which is the same in him and in others, what you have left is not an Englishman, nor a man, but some I know not what residuum, which never existed by itself, and does not so exist. If we suppose the world of relations, in which he was born and bred, never to have been, then we suppose the very essence of him not to be; if we take that away, we have taken him away."[34] The individualist framework of Christian ethics moves ethics away from the social vocabulary of the feudal/communal system into the language of individual choice and personal responsibility. Feudal Christians describe ethical issues and therefore see ethical matters in terms that are likely to have no resonance at all for individualistic Christians, though they both take themselves to be following the directives of the Sermon on the Mount.

The third framework into which Christian ethics were worked, in my view, is not so clearly spelled out by MacIntyre as it is by sociologists like Max Weber. It is the framework of capitalism. In it, commerce is the place of the moral life. MacIntyre writes, "[P]uritanism is transformed from a critique of the established order in the name of King Jesus to an endorsement of the new economic activities of the middle classes. At the end of this process economic man emerges fully fledged . . . To make one's way is to make one's way economically."[35]

Weber, of course, called this transformed puritanism "the Protestant ethic," that set of beliefs to the effect that hard work and self-discipline will be rewarded with earthly prosperity by the grace of God. The idea is that "restless, continuous, systematic work in a worldly calling"[36] is held in highest esteem by God and therefore honored by prosperity. The identification of this Christian framework conception with the Protestants is probably due to the fact that a number of Protestant sects, both in their formative years and today, profess some version of it. (There are ancient Biblical roots to the belief as well, though much of the Book of Job seems to be devoted to belittling it. Job had been a hard worker, a devout man, and a pillar of his community, still he lost his prosperity and everything that went with it because of a cosmic wager between God and Satan.)

The Protestant ethic encourages utilization of talents in commerce in order to achieve both earthly prosperity and heavenly salvation. There is a hint of this sort of thing, even, in Luther, or at least, in Luther's divorce of the secular from the religioethic side of life. But it must have been rather difficult for capitalist Christians to justify their framework with Jesus' words in the Sermon on the Mount: "Do not lay up for yourselves treasures on earth, where moth and rust consume and where thieves break in and steal, but lay up for yourselves treasures in heaven, where neither moth nor rust consumes and where thieves do not break in and steal. For where your treasure is, there will your heart be also . . . No one can serve two masters; for either he will hate the one and love the other, or he will be devoted to the one and despise the other. You cannot serve God and mammon." This last admonition is quoted by the Preacher in *Pale Rider* as an attack on the mining baron LaHood. The scene goes as follows:

> The Preacher: You can't serve God and mammon both. Mammon being money.
> LaHood (stares for a few moments at the Preacher): I opened this country, made this town what it is. I brought jobs and industry. I built an empire with my own two hands and I've never asked help from anyone. Those squatters are standing in the way of progress.
> The Preacher: Theirs or yours?

The interesting point, however, is that the independent miners in the canyon are just as much after mammon as LaHood. They are seeking their fortunes and become ecstatic with every find. One difference between them and LaHood is that he has developed hydraulic pressure technologies to virtually strip down a whole mountainside to expose nuggets. Ecological destruction, as well as human destruction, mean nothing to him in his pursuit of fortune. He is a capitalist, but not a capitalistic Christian. The loosely confederated group of independent miners, by and large, are capitalistic Christians. They, of course, need Megan's miracle to survive. Her miracle, however, is death, the Pale Rider, who though he knows and can quote Scripture, is not a Christian of any description.

The capitalistic framework of Christianity, more or less, preserves Christian ethics without the trappings of otherworldliness. No wonder it has proved so popular. The commercial world was undoubtedly a more exciting and absorbing one than the feudal system could provide for the average person, and that was probably crucial to the need for Christian ethics to adopt a different framework. When one's daily activities are routine and boring and seem, to all intents and purposes, to be without any real point, the appeal of a Kingdom of Heaven and a salvation from the ordinary is persuasive. But once one's this-worldly projects begin to absorb one's attention and energies, the concern about finding the meaning of life in some other worldly or afterlife existence drifts far into the background of one's mind. There is quite enough to occupy all of one's waking hours in the affairs of business. "Belief in a God of any specific kind becomes increasingly a formality."[37] The daily challenge of the market and commerce overwhelms spiritual concerns.

The Protestant ethic seems to have played no small role in the creation of the capital that fledgling industry needed to expand, and expanding industry was something its prescription for salvation encouraged. It also justified the accumulation of wealth by the middle class. Prosperity favors those who are self-reliant, frugal, hardworking, and rational in their decision making. Economic and social failure is the price paid by those who lack those virtues.

What we have then are at least three frameworks in which the Christian ethical doctrines and commandments are interpreted, giving rise to distinct ways of life. There are also hybrid versions, cross-pollinations of the purer types. There are individuals and groups who seem in a transitional state, holding firmly to the views of one framework but also embracing some of those of another. The Western, at least in some of the films, whether or not consciously, provides us with representatives of these various pure types and some hybrids as well. Those films offer a veritable laboratory in which to observe the interactions and clashes within the Christian perspective as well as the response of the perspective to various types of outside influence.

The townswomen of the Western, such as the women who drive Dallas out of town in *Stagecoach*, by and large, are dedicated feudal Christians. The businesspeople of the towns, in most of the films, are capitalistic Christians. A look at most of the townspeople of Hadleyville in *High Noon* should provide adequate examples of this type. When Marshal Kane enters the church to virtually beg the congregation for their help, he not so much learns that they are cowardly, as that they care more about their potential profits than they do about retribution or law and order. Some shout that they put away Frank Miller, the outlaw, once, and that they pay good money for a marshal and deputies and that keeping order and upholding the law are not their jobs: something of a "stations and duties" approach. Only one person, a woman, tries to shame the congregation into helping Kane, but she is quickly shouted down. The minister is so befuddled about what his Christianity requires that all he can say is that he cannot say what they should do. Then the real views of the townspeople are given voice when the character played by Thomas Mitchell speaks. He reminds the congregation that the town's industrial prospects, its capitalistic projects, will be set back for years if a gunfight erupts in the streets of their town. He urges Kane to run away so that Miller will have no one to fight. It would be better for the town, better for business.

The homesteaders in *Shane*, and the independent miners of *Pale Rider*, also fall in the category of capitalistic Christians. So do the farmers and ranchers of most of John Ford's films. Pure individualist Christians are a bit harder to find, though perhaps the minister in *The Ballad of Cable Hogue* is a committed Christian individualist, played (by David Warner) for the humor of his religious position, of course. Also, it might not be a great stretch to say that even some of the heroes of Westerns are, to some degree at least, individualistic Christians, albeit lapsed to a significant degree. I wonder about J. B. Books. Still, the westerner's commitment to vengeance as a justification for violent action, and his refusal to submit to most of the admonitions of the Sermon on the Mount, marks him more as an outsider of any of the Christian frameworks, even if on some points he may share a concern or two with a Christian.

The interesting people in the Western with respect to this analysis of Christian ethics frameworks are the heroines, the women that Boetticher said were important because of what they represented. What do they represent? None of them seem to be dedicated capitalistic Christians. Many do seem to be somewhat feudally inclined, at least at the beginning of the films. Community is important to them, but it is not the thing they care most about. They are ready to pull up stakes to avoid serious confrontations with the villains. Both Marion (of *Shane*) and Sarah (of *Pale Rider*) more than suggest it and are rebuffed by their capitalistic male counterparts. Mrs. Jorgenson (of *The Searchers*) will stick it out in the desert, but she would prefer no conflict, and certainly none motivated by vengeance. Still, the heroines are not, and do not usually transform into, full-fledged individualist Christians. There are, however, some notable exceptions. The wife of the hotel owner in *High Plains Drifter* undergoes a change from a hybrid capitalistic/feudal Christian into an individualistic one after she spends a night with the Clint Eastwood character. She is more than willing to forgive the Eastwood character, if not her capitalistic Christian husband. Sarah, however, after also sleeping with an Eastwood character, the Preacher, does not undergo a thorough transformation into an individualist. She retains vestiges of the feudal. She will marry Hull and live a rather ordinary life. One could speculate about the impact on Bond Rogers's feudal version of Christianity after her week-long encounter with J. B. Books, but it would only be speculation. Jane Withersteen in *Riders of the Purple Sage* (1996) (played by Amy Madigan) from the very beginning is seen as a hybrid of a capitalistic and an individualistic Christian. The individualistic side of her ends up dominating, if, indeed, she retains any Christian framework by the end of the film. Her savior is not Jesus Christ, but Lassiter, a violent gunman. In the same film is to be found a male hybrid that is prominent in Westerns: The leaders of the Mormon Church are feudal/capitalistic

Christians, though a considerable amount of their Christianity, in any form, has been replaced with the sheer meanness that both greed and religious fanaticism can generate. The shopkeepers, mine company executives, and the hotel owner of *High Plains Drifter* are hybrids of the same sort. They are committed to the hierarchy of the feudal system while engaged in what they believe to be the Christian-ordained pursuit of personal profit.

In those films in which the homesteaders and the shopkeepers are juxtaposed to cattlemen who are living the ways of the past and desperately trying to preserve what once was, though the eventual struggle must inevitably go to the capitalistic Christians who have enlisted the hero in their cause, we are generally shown that the westerner feels a genuine sympathy for the cattlemen. In *Shane*, for example, the Rikers are not portrayed as incarnations of evil. They are westerners, outside of the Christian ethical frameworks, who cannot cope with the changes that the homesteaders' version of capitalistic Christianity has brought to the valley they (the cattlemen) fought so long to turn into productive open range. They recognize a "soulmate" in Shane and invite him to join them. But he has committed to the homesteaders. Moments before the final shoot-out in Grafton's saloon, Riker has the following conversation with Shane:

> Riker: I got no quarrel with you, Shane.
> Shane: That's too bad.
> Riker: oo bad?
> Shane: Yeah. You've lived too long. Your kinda days are over.
> Riker: My days? What about yours, gunfighter?
> Shane: The difference is, I know it.
> Riker: All right, so we'll all turn in our six-guns to the bartender and we'll all start hoein' spuds.
> Shane: Not quite yet.

The final shoot-out is less a glorious moment than a downright sad one. Only the homesteaders, who are represented at the scene by the hero-worshipping witness Little Joey, will benefit from its outcome.

I suspect that one of the reasons that the heroine in the Western is able, despite typically great inner struggles, and outer ones as well, to accept and even endorse the behavior of the westerner, is that her Christianity is to some not-insignificant degree individualistic, and the individualism of the framework is threatening to overcome any of the ethical elements that have been fitted into it. She can be tempted more to the westerner's outlook on life than her capitalistic and feudal cousins. She, at some level that the westerner eventually mines, understands her Christian commitments in psychological terms. She can divorce the secular world and its law from her conception of salvation. Catherine (in *Will Penny*) seems bent on trying to do that, but Will is uncooperative. For her, the Lutheran salvation by grace alone is understood as meaning that nothing humans do on this earth is good, that it is all sinful. And she is sometimes able even to join the westerner, if only for a few moments of violent action, as does Susannah MacAskill (of *The Quick and The Dead*; 1987), Amy Kane (of *High Noon*), Evie Peel (of *Conagher*), and Jane Withersteen (of *Riders of the Purple Sage*; 1996).

In the end, she, better than anyone else, understands the westerner. In *The Quick and the Dead*, for example, the following closing dialogue occurs between Conn Vallian the westerner, the male MacAskill the easterner, and MacAskill's wife Susannah, after the MacAskills have gunned down the villains:

> Vallian: Damn, you folks are quick, but you still got to remember to watch your back. . . .
> MacAskill: You've angered me. You've embarrassed me. You've shamed me. You've certainly worried the hell out of me. But through it all, there's something I've always responded to. There's a kindness in you Vallian. That's what I'll miss. . . .
> Vallian: You've got a little sand there, MacAskill. Nourish it and you might turn out to be quite a westerner. . . .
> Susannah (to Vallian): I hope you find a good life.
> Vallian: My life ain't that bad, ma'am. To me, it's the best, always the best.
> Susannah: I guess wild things don't do too well in a garden.
> Vallian: Wild things gotta be free. (He rides off into the mountains.)

Perhaps she and only she also recognizes that she represents everything that ultimately will destroy the westerner, that she is what for him must be the corruption of his lifestyle and the loss of all he cares about. She is civilization, or at least its version of goodness, a goodness that in the end is anathema to his existence. Marion (in *Shane*) recognizes this and her husband Joe totally fails to grasp it. He tells Marion, as he prepares to go into town to face down the Rikers and Wilson, that he knows that if he is killed, that Shane will take care of her, probably better than he can. Marion knows that Shane is not capable of the lifestyle she requires, but Joe is. Shane is a westerner, a gunfighter, a killer. Shane and Joe fight over who will face the Rikers, and Marion screams and frets and covers her eyes throughout their fight. When it is over and Shane has knocked Joe unconscious, she says to Shane:

Marion: You were through with gunfighting.

Shane: I've changed my mind. . . .

Marion: And we'll never see you again?

Shane: Never's a long time.

Marion: Please, Shane. Please take care of yourself . . . (then to Little
    Joey who cannot understand why Shane has hit his father over the
    head with a gun and is on his way to fight the Rikers and Wilson):
    Shane did what he had to do, Joey.

Marion realizes both that Shane and only Shane is capable of saving her
family from the vicious Rikers and their gunman, and that by endorsing
Shane's mission of violence she is deserting her deepest-held principles and
beliefs. Nonetheless, she does so, and, in fact, despite the befuddlement of
her son, she thanks Shane for ending a fistfight between himself and her
husband Joe, started over who should take on the Rikers, by the apparently
cowardly act of bashing her husband over the head with his pistol. (It may
not be a coincidence that Marion, a variant of Mary, is married to Joseph
and that their family's savior is a cold-blooded gunfighter.)

VII

There are two types of Christian ethical conflicts in Westerns: the internecine ones and the ones between some version of Christian ethics and outsiders, westerners who have "gone bad" or are so devoted to the past of
the West that they made "with their own two hands" that they are desperately trying to stave off the future they see before them. It is a future in
which they are reduced to myth and footnotes in history and are being
replaced by the easterner and values they tried to escape earlier in their lives
and thoroughly despise. The internecine conflicts may involve different
frameworks for the ethics or different interpretations of the admonitions of
Christianity within the same framework. In *Pale Rider*, for example, the
conflict, as identified by the Preacher, is "whose progress?" LaHood's or
that of the independent miners? It is not between progress, understood in
capitalistic terms, and the preservation of the wilderness, although that conflict does provide a sort of subplot, allowing the westerner to express his
identity with the wilderness, especially the mountains out of which he
rode, by blowing up LaHood's strip-mining operation.

When the conflict is internecine and within the same basic framework,
one of the protagonists has inevitably trespassed the bounds of the Christian
ethical requirements. In the case of capitalistic Christianity, somewhere
along the way in the accumulation of profit, a line gets crossed into greed,

a sin. Where that line is to be drawn was an issue that exercised Locke and other prophets of the profit motive. In the Western's version of this, the villain's motivation is owning all of the valley or all of the businesses in town, while the capitalistic Christians are only out to make a reasonable profit. The westerner comes to the aid of the homesteaders, townspeople, or independent miners, not because he favors capitalistic Christianity, but because they are overmatched by the resources the greedy villain can bring to bear against them. The westerner's cause is never the cause of profit, nor is it for a proper or just distribution of the resources. He enters the fight as a sort of offset for the balance of power, and usually he does so reluctantly and finally because there is a woman involved to whom he believes either he has to prove something or requires his protection despite her association with commitments and cares he steadfastly rejects.

Sometimes, as with LaHood and Braxton (of *The Missouri Breaks*), the villain is a former westerner who has converted to the cares of easterner Christianity (usually of the capitalistic variety), though he is still rough around the edges and is liable to use westerner ways to bring about easterner goals. The character of Frank (played by Henry Fonda) in *Once Upon a Time in the West*, is an especially good example of a westerner who not only has corrupted his western cares, but has adopted those of a greedy easterner. He becomes more despicable than, say, Wilson (in *Shane*), whose corrupted western values allow him to hire out his considerable talents as a gunfighter in the cause of westerners trying to prevent the death of their West.

In the category of the internecine Christian conflicts are to be found *Pale Rider, Riders of the Purple Sage*, and *Once Upon a Time in the West* (though the later is so complex that it contains both types). Among the outer conflicts, those between various Christian ethical frameworks and outsiders, are *Shane, The Quick and the Dead, The Tall T, High Plains Drifter*, and *Hombre*.

The westerner is contemptuous of all that easterners, their culture, their religion, and their legal system claim for themselves. As well as any other westerner, Ben Rumson in *Paint Your Wagon* expresses that contempt when he "sings":

Rumson: In come the people and gum it up good.
   The first thing you know . . .
They civilize what's pretty, by puttin' up a city
Where nothin' that's pretty can grow.
They muddy up the winter and civilize it inter
A place too uncivilized even for snow.

The first thing you know.
    They civilize left, they civilize right,
'Til nothin' is left and nothin' is right.
They civilize freedom, 'til no one is free . . .
The first thing you know.

But the westerners may also fear that the easterners are the very sources of their own potential corruption, and no more so than in those temptations laid out by those good Christian women. The faces of Shane and Conn Vallian at the end of their films seem to express, at least in part, relief that they have escaped temptation one more time. They ride back to their mountains, into the West, toward a death that casts a shadow over the meaning and worth of their lives, unforgiven, unforgiving, and most assuredly not to be numbered among the meek who will inherit the earth.

NOTES

1. Tompkins, *West of Everything*, 32.

2. Ibid., chap. 1.

3. Ibid., 42–43, quoted in Carl Degler, *At Odds* (New York, 1980).

4. Ibid., 45.

5. Ibid., 33.

6. Philip French, *Westerns*, rev. ed., (New York, 1977), 63.

7. The Sermon is found in Matthew, chapters 5–7.

8. St. Augustine, *The City of God*, trans. Walsh, Zema, Monahan, and Honan (Garden City, N.J., 1958), chap. 14, 278–79.

9. Ibid., chap. 22, 519.

10. St. Ireneaus, *Adversus Haereses*, trans. D. J. Unger (New York, 1992).

11. Earlier, however, Jesus maintains that he has not come to abolish the law, presumably Mosaic law. He says, "For truly, I say to you, till heaven and earth pass away, not an iota, not a dot, will pass from the law until all is accomplished. Whoever then relaxes one of the least of these commandments and teaches men so, shall be called least in the kingdom of heaven; but he who does them and teaches them shall be called great in the kingdom of heaven." The reference of "these commandments" in this passage is rather unclear to me. Does it refer to the commandments that are a part of the old code? Or is the referent the slew of beatitudes that just precedes the remark? My assumption is that Jesus refers to the commandments in the law, because of the expression "whoever then . . . ". If that is the case, then the forgiveness requirement of a few verses on, is, at least apparently, in conflict with this admonition. Perhaps one is supposed to forgive someone of his trespass, say the poking out of an eye, while one pokes out the offender's eye.

12. Joseph Butler, *Fifteen Sermons* (London, 1726), sermon, "Upon Resentment."

13. Jeffrie Murphy and Jean Hampton, *Forgiveness and Mercy* (Cambridge, 1988), 16.

14. Peter Strawson, "Freedom and Resentment," *Proceedings of the British Academy* (1962).

15. Murphy and Hampton, *Forgiveness and Mercy*, 17.

16. Ibid., 19.

17. Ibid., 37.

18. Ibid., 85.

19. John Kekes, *Facing Evil* (Princeton, N.J., 1990).

20. J. L. Austin, *Philosophical Papers*, 2d Ed. (Oxford, 1970), 176.

21. Tompkins, *West of Everything*, 52.

22. Quoted by Tuska, *The American West in Film*, 224.

23. Tompkins, *West of Everything*, 62.

24. Alasdair MacIntyre, *A Short History of Ethics* (New York, 1966), chap. 9.

25. Ibid., 115.

26. Ibid., 116.

27. Walter Ullmann, *The Individual and Society* (Baltimore, Md., 1966), 44.

28. For a fuller account of this aspect of art in the period, see James Burke, *The Day the Universe Changed* (London, 1985), chap. 3.

29. See MacIntyre, *A Short History of Ethics*, chap. 10.

30. Ibid., 122.

31. Ibid., 127.

32. Ibid., 125–26.

33. Rudyard Kipling, "Tomlinson" in *The One Volume Kipling* (Garden City, N.J., 1932), 28–29.

34. F. H. Bradley, *Ethical Studies*, (1876; Oxford, 1989), 166.

35. MacIntyre, *A Short History of Ethics*, 150.

36. Max Weber, *The Protestant Ethic and the Spirit of Capitalism*, trans. T. Parsons (New York, 1958), 172.

37. MacIntyre, *A Short History of Ethics*, 150.

· 3 ·

THE SHADOW OF DEATH

I

After the climactic gunfight of *Once Upon a Time in the West*, the outlaw Cheyenne, played by Jason Robards, has the following conversation with the heroine Jill, played by Claudia Cardinale, whom he has been coaching with respect to her role in the town that is being built by the new railroad tracks:

> Cheyenne: I'm not the right man, and neither is he.
> Jill: Maybe not, but it doesn't matter.
> Cheyenne: You don't understand, Jill. People like that have something inside, something to do with *death*. If that fellow lives, coming through that door, he'll pick up his gear and say 'adios.'

And, of course, "that fellow," Charles Bronson's character Harmonica does exactly that.

All westerners have something inside that has to do with death, and it is not just because they live and die by the gun. It is because the westerner cares about death, his own death. It is extremely important to him. It focuses and frames his world view and the ethics to which he is committed. Death, in no small measure, is what his life is all about. In *Will Penny*, a film that is, in large measure, about death, the following conversations occur:

> Dutchy (who is gut shot): Maybe he's right, what he says. I'll die, die before we get there.
> Will: No.
> Dutchy: We waited a long time for a drink of whiskey . . . I'd like to have a sure drink here rather than a maybe drink later on . . . Am I going to die?
> Will: It happens to all of us, Dutchy.
> Dutchy: Oh, no Will. You know what I mean. Is now my time?

Will: I don't know, Dutchy. How the hell do I know?
Dutchy: There's a whole lot I ain't done yet, cowboyin' around. It hurts
   like hell . . . I'm only twenty-seven years old.

The most clearly anti-Christian element of Westerns and the conception on which most of the Western's ethical precepts are ultimately
grounded is its view of death. For the Christian and many of the leading
philosophers in our intellectual tradition, a person's life does not end in the
death of that person. Death, from the earliest stages of Christianity, was
believed to have been "conquered" by resurrection, resurrection of the
body, and by eternal life. After death, the true Christian, according to St.
Paul, can expect to survive in a celestial body and look forward to deathlessness, eternal life in Heaven.[1] Paul writes to the Corinthians:

> Just as all die in Adam, so in Christ all will be brought to life . . . If the
> dead are not going to be raised, then let us eat and drink, for tomorrow
> we shall be dead . . . Someone may ask: How are dead people raised, and
> what sort of body do they have when they come? How foolish! What
> you sow must die before it is given new life; and what you sow is not
> the body that is to be, but only a bare grain, of wheat I dare say, or some
> other kind; it is God who gives it the sort of body that he has chosen for
> it, and for each kind of seed its own kind of body . . . There are heavenly
> bodies and earthly bodies; the heavenly have a splendor of their own,
> and the earthly a different splendor . . . what is sown is perishable, but
> what is raised is imperishable . . . what is sown is a natural body, and
> what is raised is a spiritual body . . . The trumpet is going to sound, then
> the dead will be raised imperishable, and we shall be changed, because
> this perishable nature of ours must put on imperishability, this mortal
> nature must put on immortality . . . Death *is swallowed up in victory. Death,
> where is your victory? Death, where is your sting?*[2]

Unrepentant sinners, of course, can expect an eternity of suffering in Hell.
The central point, however, seems to be that the life of a person continues
or is reconstituted in some fashion after biological death. It is unclear from
Paul whether this is a matter of personal survival, though his insistence that,
if resurrection were not the case, we would join the Epicureans and eat
and drink suggests personal survival. In any event, as Christian theology on
the subject of death became more and more influenced by Platonic thinking, the ideas that there is a life after death for everyone, that the self of this
life continues into the next, that there is a causal link with major ethical
consequences between what one does in one's life in this world and what
one will do in one's life in the "next world" became commonplace Christian theology.

It is not difficult to see why the post-first-century Christians would opt to modify the Pauline position. Paul clearly expected the resurrection of the dead to be just around the corner, and, of course centuries came and went without its occurrence. Paul's conception of resurrection also seems to be a deliberate rejection of the Platonic spiritualistic, immortal, soul-centered account of afterlife in favor of what might be called a materialist conception of the person. For Paul, we are bodies. First terrestrial and then, by the will and grace of God, celestial, but always bodies. He does not talk about souls.

Gilbert Murray maintains that the reason Paul avoided Platonic talk was because his audience could only grasp the doctrine of immortality in the physical body version.[3] Others, like Jacques Choron, argue that Paul offered the resurrection theory because he believed in the idea of deathlessness in the same body.[4] The whole idea, however, as Tertullian noted, both does not make sense and is impossible, the very reasons Tertullian then cites for why it is both believable and certain ("*certum est, quia impossibile est.*"[5]) With arguments as persuasive as that, little wonder it became so popular!

Platonic souls were a more attractive location for the essence of a person, of personal identity, and of personality. They better fitted into what was, apparently, a more persuasive way of understanding death: as a kind of transportation of the person from one world to the next, something the resurrection of the body idea resists. Bodies, after all, rot and disintegrate, and the relationship between a new celestial body and a rotting terrestrial one was not altogether clear to the later Christians despite Paul's metaphor of the seed.[6] In any event, what Paul and the later Christian writers do insist upon is that death is not to be feared by the true believer, that it is some sort of interim stage through which a person passes. It has no sting. And better things, at least for the Christian, are ahead.

II

In Westerns, proving one's manhood or one's integrity, which pretty much comes to the same thing, at the risk of death or at the point of death, sustains the plots. The conception of death that is adopted, and even glorified, in Westerns, structures and delimits the ethics endorsed in the genre. The favored conception of death is a clear and, it seems fair to say, deliberate rejection of the standard Christian conception. In Westerns, death is understood by the main characters [at least the hero and the leading villain(s)] to be the utterly inevitable annihilation of a life. There is no promise or hope of an afterlife. Death brings it all to a close. The sting of death is very real. Its victory is the victory of ending a person's existence and all that person ever was or will be.

Will Penny finds a dead cowboy on the range and rides into the Flat Iron Ranch with the corpse. He explains to the foreman and some of the hands:

> Will: I figured he bucked off and wrapped up the whole ball of wax right there.
> Hand: Old Claude was a pretty good horsebacker.
> Will: If you say so. I never had the pleasure.
> Alex (the foreman): What brings you up here?
> Will: You the stud duck?
> Alex: That's right. Old Claude was a pretty good cowpuncher.
> Hand: Mighty good man all around.
> Will: Well sure. That's always the way, ain't it?
> Alex: What's always the way?
> Will: Let a man die, right away he's good old Claude. How was he before he bucked out?

Christian funeral rituals, where religion confronts death, in Westerns are typically mocked as silly wastes of words, time, and effort. Insofar as there are usually a number of dead bodies in the films, the opportunities for such derision are frequent. In *Pale Rider,* after a miner is shot down in the streets of town, rather than conducting a funeral, the Preacher rides off to strap on his guns and tells the miners to bury the deceased. He has no interest in conducting a service. In *Will Penny* we hear:

> Station owner: Belly shot out here, he's a dead man. He'll bleed himself out long before you get him to Alford. Best thing you can do for him, pilgrim, is make him rest easy while he waits for the end. Anything he drinks is on the house. We can bury him out back, away from the hogs. It won't cost much. I'll even carve him a nice head marker. Twenty five dollars sound about right to you? Ground's kinda hard this time of year.

In the opening of *Paint Your Wagon*, Ben Rumson conducts a mocking funeral for a prospector who has been killed in a wagon accident. He calls to a God he does not really believe exists: "What I'm trying to say, God, is you don't seem to have no particular pity for your children when they livin', so that's why we're askin' ya to be a little kinder to 'em when they dead." Then he spots gold dust in the freshly dug grave and shouts, "I stake this claim. Haul 'im up." The body is pulled up and tossed aside. There's gold to be mined, a fortune to be made.

After Jason Robards as Cable Hogue, in *The Ballad of Cable Hogue*, has had to kill a cowboy who tries to avoid paying for a drink at Cable's waterhole, he says to the corpse, "Appears to me you've been seventeen kinds of a damn fool, not that it seems to bother you."

John Wayne's character Tom Dunson, in *Red River*, mutters over the graves of the men he kills at various points in the film, "The Lord giveth, the Lord taketh away." And, as Tompkins notes, "we are supposed to perceive the ridiculousness of believing in a divine Providence that has obviously had no part in deciding the fate of the poor chumps."[7] One of the cowhands in the same film says, "Plantin' 'n' readin', plantin' 'n' readin'. Fill a man full of lead, stick him in the ground, and then read words at him. Why when you've killed a man, why try to read the Lord in as a partner in the job?" The same Biblical passage favored by Dunson is used with venom by Preacher Quint, the villain of *Will Penny*. He and his band have set upon Will and beaten him to a pulp, stabbed him, and stripped him to his long johns. One of Quint's sons wants to kill Penny there and then, but the old man wants Will to "die hard. A mighty long time and then he'll be dead." Then Quint intones with mock solemnity over the beaten body of Will, "Ashes to ashes, dust to dust. The Lord giveth and the Lord taketh away. Blessed be the name of the Lord."

In *Cowboy*, the trailboss Tom Reese (played by Glenn Ford) is confronted with conducting a funeral for a trailhand killed by a snake bite. He asks the other cowhands, "Anybody know the right words?" No one does. A similar scene takes place in *Dead Man's Walk*. There is another funeral on the trail and the question is asked of the cowboys, "What are the words?" "It's something about green pastures," one of them says. There is a general muttering about green pastures and then silence. They shrug and cover up the body. In *Cowboy*, Reese offers the following eulogy:

> Reese: Something like this happens, people start askin' how come it happened. Was it his fault? Was it somebody else's fault? Well, that isn't for us to say. You see, we don't know all the answers. All we know is that a man is dead and that's that. But in the long run, I don't think it would make any difference anyhow. I mean, if it hadn't been a snake that got him, it would have been a steer, or a Comanche, or it might have been his horse stumbled in a prairie dog hole some dark night. He was a good man with cattle. He always did the best he knew how. I hope somebody can say the same over me. All right, throw the dirt over him.

In *The Searchers*, at the funeral of his brother and his brother's wife Martha, the woman he himself loved, Ethan Edwards interrupts the singing of the hymn (John Ford's all purpose "Shall We Gather At The River") with "Put an 'Amen' to it." There's revenge to be taken. Action, death-dealing, not religion is called for. A few minutes later in the film, Edwards shoots out the eyes of a dead Comanche.

> Reverend/Captain Clayton: What good did that do you?
> Edwards: By what you preach, none. But what that Comanch believes, he ain't got no eyes, he can't enter the spirit land. He has to wander forever between the winds. You get it, Reverend.

One funeral, that of Ethan's brother and his brother's wife, is juxtaposed to the discovery of the Comanche burial. At the first, Ethan disrupts the ritual, bringing it to a premature close. At the second, he desecrates the corpse and thereby ensures the failure of the Comanche ritual to achieve its purpose. Of course, within *The Searchers* the latter act has a much deeper meaning: it foreshadows Ethan's own future. He will never be restored to a home life and a proper position in the community. Although he is condemning the Comanche warrior to wander forever between the winds, that is exactly what his own fate will be, and it will be the fate of most of the other westerners as well.

In *Lonesome Dove*, Clara interrupts Chollo's digging of the grave for her husband's body for a brief rumination on death.

> Clara: Sometimes it seems like gravediggin's all we do around here, don't it, Chollo? What do you think happens when we die?
> Chollo: Not so much, you are just dead.
> Clara: Maybe it's not as big a change as we think. Maybe you just go back to where you lived or near family or wherever you was happiest. Only you're just a spirit now and you don't have the troubles that the living have.
> Chollo: I don't know. Maybe so.
> Clara: Well.

Her last line is uttered more as a sigh of regret that Chollo was probably right with his first answer than as an indication that she thinks she has uncovered some deep mystery of death. You are just dead!

In *Hondo*, the hero explains death with the simple clipped westerner's way of getting to the core of the matter: "Everybody gets dead. It was his turn."

After gunning down two bounty hunters, the Clint Eastwood title character of *The Outlaw Josey Wales* responds to the worry of the young man with whom he is riding that they should take time to bury the corpses, "The hell with them fellas. Buzzards got to eat the same as worms." He then mockingly anoints the head of one of his victims by spitting tobacco juice on it before riding off. Later in the film, Josey Wales mutters while strapping the corpse of his young friend to a horse, "This boy was brought up in a time of blood and dying, never questioned a bit of it, never turned his back on his folks or his kind. I rode with him; I got no complaints." Then he sends the horse galloping off into a camp of pursuers to serve as a distraction so he can avoid capture. Importantly, Josey Wales's funeral oration never mentions God nor talks of the young man now being better off in a celestial afterlife. There is no attempt at consolation, no invocation of divine will to explain events. Its focus is purely and simply on the lived life now concluded and what was made of it. It praises the deceased for having the virtues of a westerner: courage in the face of blood and dying and, importantly, not questioning a bit of it, taking life as it comes. It honors the deceased for remaining steadfast, and it caps the life evaluation with a simple resignation to the whole process of a life that always terminates in death: "I got no complaints." There is no appeal to God to find the deceased worthy, and surely Josey Wales does not believe that the fact that he has no complaints constitutes a recommendation to a heavenly court. However, friendship and loyalty, major virtues of the Western, get their due: "I rode with him." Missing is any reference to the deceased as having by nature intrinsic worth. What counts is how he lived, "he never turned his back on his folks or his kind," not that he has a soul or spirit that is precious in itself and worthy of divine or human consideration.

In *Lonesome Dove*, Captain Woodrow Call carves a grave marker for Josh Deets that, in the same vein as Josey Wales's eulogy for his companion, reads, "Josh Deets, served with me thirty years, fought in twenty-one engagements with the Comanche and the Kiowa, cheerful in all weathers, never shirked a task. Splendid behavior." The life is summarized, but there is no mention of an afterlife, a soul, or anything of the kind.

Similar sentiments are expressed by John Wayne, as Will Anderson in *The Cowboys*, when he buries a young boy who has been trampled to death by cattle. His only words are, "Sometimes it's hard to understand the drift of things. This was a good boy. He'd a been a good man. But he didn't get the chance. Death can come for you anyplace, anytime. It's never welcome, but if you've done all you can do and it's your best, in a way, I guess, you're ready for him. Go on back to camp."

The world of the Western is a world of work and death without God. That is crucial to understanding its conception of virtue and ethics, and the attendant values it teaches. Remember Megan's prayer at the beginning of *Pale Rider.* It would seem that even young women doubt whether God exists. Megan's savior is not "Life Everlasting," but Death. Early in that film the miner, Hull, who is engaged to Megan's mother, observes the Preacher's body is laced with bullet wounds, most of which should have been fatal. Indeed, they were fatal! The Preacher is *Death*, as Megan seems to sense from first sighting him while reading Revelation. He is Death on a mission of death, the Pale Rider. At the end of the film, as the Preacher rides back into the snowy mountains after slaughtering more than a dozen people, Megan cries out to him that she loves him (loves Death?). She had begged him to have sex with her, to initiate her into adulthood. After all, it is the personal experience of evil and death that ends innocence.[8] He refused, but certainly not on spiritual grounds. The Preacher is no spirit or angel. He is very much a human, a man who spends a final night in bed with Megan's mother Sarah, gaining in the liaison a representative of Christianity's acquiescence in his mission of death.

At the end of *Hombre*, the Paul Newman lead character tells us, "We all die, it's just a question of when." Then he is shot to death.

III

World views with respect to death, human death, can be: (a) death-accepting, (b) death-denying, (c) death-defying, or (d) a combination of (b) and (c). The Christian perspective is, at its core, death-defying. By that I mean that death, for the Christian, as previously noted, is regarded as having been overcome and is overcomeable by true devotees. People, or at least Christians, die, but not in the normal sense of that term. In fact, the language typically used when talking about death by both Christians and those embued with popular culture avoids the terms "die," "dead," and "death" like the plague.

We do not talk about people dying. They get lost, they leave, they fall asleep. How odd it is to say of one's mother, "we lost her last year." How careless of us! I suppose the idea is that although we do not exactly know where she now is, that she is somewhere, and we might, sometime in the future, find her. I suppose it is comforting to think that someone we cherished is only lost and not annihilated. What is lost might be retrieved, found someplace we never thought to look. My mother died when I was five years old. I remember very little of the funeral, but one incident remains etched on my memory, probably because other people who were there reminded me of it for some time after the event. A woman came up to me and said in the most consoling way she could muster, "I'm so sorry you lost your mother." I responded without a moment of consideration, "She's not lost, she's dead. They just buried her." A moment of awkward silence followed, then the woman shrugged and turned to other more mature mourners.

"She left us over a year ago," conveys something of the same conception of death. She's on a trip, a journey. She took off, but she might return. There is something of the trip idea in "passed on" or "passed over." The sleeping euphemism also conjures up death-defying images of rising on some bright cheery day in another, hopefully better, place.

Micheal Kearl has noted that "We speak of death when we don't mean it, and when we do mean it we use euphemisms."[9] That practice carries over from Christianity to the dominant strains in our popular culture, but our popular culture, probably because the thrust of much of it is focused on the cult of youth that dominates our commercial lives, is also death-denying. In that sense it is surprisingly like ancient and contemporary primitive cultures. From the youngest years we are provided with images of what should be death, but turns out to be nothing at all, not even a bad bruise. Death scenes are cartooned, whether in cartoons in which one of the characters is being bashed or blown up every few minutes or in feature films in which whole towns are exploded, people are horribly mutilated, etc., and yet there is no stench of death about it. It is all so antiseptic and unreal, despite the makeup artist's talents in spreading fake blood everywhere. Death is fun in the most popular elements of popular culture, for example in the action/adventure genre of film. It is not really a serious matter. It is generally accompanied with witty, joking remarks and an enormous amount of unnecessary firepower, overkill. The hero not only needs two machine guns, assorted other weapons, grenades, rocket-launchers, and, if he is Arnold Schwartznegger, a helicopter, an atomic bomb, and a Harrier jump jet. All to kill more spectacularly, though no one really "gets dead." The plots always seem to require what seems like an unending stream of "bad guy's henchmen" for the hero to dispatch in a multitude of ever more outrageous ways. And, of course, the hero, though scratched and bruised a bit, comes through it all smiling. Though captured by the villain three or four times in the film, for some unfathomable reason, except to sustain the cliff-hanger story line, the villain never chooses to kill the hero in the simplest possible way: by shooting him in the head. This is certainly not due to a lack of guns available in the bad guy's camp. It is all just a cartoon. Jack Wilson, the gunfighter in *Shane*, would just shoot him down. End of picture.

Popular entertainers live out in their offscreen, offstage lives the death-denying/defying syndrome for the rest of us by filling the pages of the tabloids, the newspapers, and the television news with their exploits. And when one of them does die of an overdose or a sexually transmitted disease, it is all swept quickly aside and others jump into his or her place in the headlines and the gossip columns. On local television news broadcasts the rule seems to be, "If it bleeds, it leads." But again, there is no attempt to confront death, to understand it. The news is but an extension of the cartoonish shows that dominate the airwaves.

The death-defying basic tenets of Christianity underwent changes as the conceptual framework of the religion's ethics and world view shifted. Kearl provides a useful summary of what was involved and the markers that indicate the changes. He writes:

> Beginning in the twelfth century, attitudes toward death began metamorphosing with the emergence of individualism. In the context of the plagues, individuals not only became conscious of the brevity and fragility of their lives, understanding existence as a stay of execution, but they also became aware of their own unique selves and in so doing discovered their own deaths. A life was no longer subsumed within the collective destiny of the group (hence the fading of the vendetta system, as kin members were no longer seen to be functionally equivalent) but became viewed as a biography, each moment of which would be judged by Christ after death. . . . Death, not life, became the natural force that one had to master . . . To assist in this mastery, an instructional manual on the art of dying, entitled *Ars Moriendi,* was to be a best-seller for two centuries. With the concurrent rise of the Reformation, salvation once again became conditional upon the quality of one's life, and hell replaced death as the primary fear.[10]

Salvation for the Christian, of course, involves afterlife, hence the concern about Hell. In effect, if you believe that you are an immortal soul, your prudential concerns, at least, will direct your attention to insuring that the longest time you will spend: eternity, will be as well-off as possible. Death becomes just another moment in the biography of your soul, one, apparently, that the soul experiences as a journey down a tunnel and toward or through some incredibly bright white light, if you believe those pop culture accounts of the process.

In *Hombre* this whole Christian program is ridiculed. The wife of Dr. Favor, an embezzling Indian agent, has been captured by a murderous gang of outlaws and has been tied to a rail at a deserted mine in the broiling Arizona sun. She will only be released in exchange for the money Favor has stolen. Favor, other passengers, and the driver of the stagecoach are in an old mine shack above the place where Mrs. Favor has been tied. No one in the party is willing to risk her rescue or to trade the money for her. Her cries for help to her husband become weaker and weaker as the heat exhausts her energy and the sun blisters her skin. Mendez, the coach driver, talks to Dr. Favor as they look down the hillside at the dying Mrs. Favor.

> Mendez: God sees this, and if we live, we must live in fear of Him. At least that's what they frightened me with when I was a child.
> Favor: Don't be frightened, Mr. Mendez. There is no God.
> Mendez: Not in either of us, perhaps.
> Favor: Not anywhere.
> Mendez: Nothing, Dr. Favor?
> Favor: Nothing.
> Mendez: You're sure? No reward in Heaven?
> Favor: Why lie to ourselves?
> Mendez: Or Hell then? A little bit of Hell, maybe?
> Favor: Oh yes, there's Hell.

The implication, of course, is that they are currently in Hell, the only Hell they will ever experience. Neither afterlife nor God are prerequisites for Hell. There is plenty of Hell in the barren, dead desert landscapes of the Western.

Alan Harrington nicely captures the contemporary attitude that developed out of the cultural death-denying that marks our age. He writes, "Death is an imposition on the human race and no longer acceptable. Men and women have all but lost their ability to accommodate themselves to personal extinction; they must now proceed . . . to kill death; put an end to mortality as a certain consequence of being born."[11]

The westerner is death-accepting ("We all die, it's just a question of when."). He adopts a two-pronged conception of death. Death is inevitable for us all ("Everybody gets dead. It was his turn."), and it is the annihilation of the person. The only thing related to or identifiable with the deceased that lives after his or her death are the memories the living have of the deceased, and those memories are framed in purely nonspiritual terms, in terms of the actions and the attitudes of the deceased while alive: "Splendid behavior!" "Cheerful in all weathers!" "I rode with him; I got no complaints."

IV

There are, then, two distinct steps involved in adopting the westerner's conception of death. First, one must accept the inevitability of death and,

second, one must come to understand that at death a person is totally annihilated. Christians make the first step and refuse to take the second. According to a number of standard accounts in the anthropological literature,
primitive cultures, at least in their early stages, take neither step. Choron
writes: "For the primitive, . . . death is the result of the action or malign
influence of an enemy in either human or spiritual form: one can be killed,
or magic can induce a deadly sickness. But for these hostile acts, no one
would ever die."[12] Choron reasons that because what we call ancient cultures felt it necessary to create myths to explain the origin of death, in the
cultures that preceded them, "death was not considered a necessary attri-
bute of the human condition."[13] Even in the Old Testament, Adam and
Eve through their own acts bring about God's wrath and the curse of death.
In other cultures, the gods send death to humans more out of jealousy of
the humans than because of some acts of human irreverence or disobedience. There is even a hint of such a divine concern in the Biblical account.
It should not be forgotten that there were two important trees in the Garden of Eden. One, the violated Tree of the Knowledge of Good and Evil,
and the other the Tree of Life. Once the prohibition against the first was
broken, the rather puzzling text reads: "Then the Lord God said, 'Behold,
the man has become like one of us, knowing good and evil; and now lest
he put forth his hand and take also of the tree of life, and eat and live
forever.'—therefore the Lord God sent him forth from the Garden of Eden,
to till the ground from which he was taken."[14] In effect, the Tree of the
Knowledge of Good and Evil turns out to be the Tree of Death. In fact,
God, Eve reports to the serpent, told Adam and Eve that if they even touch
the Tree of the Knowledge of Good and Evil, they will die.

After primitives realized that everyone does die, the standard conjecture is that the idea that death is annihilation must have crept into their
thinking as they became more and more aware of decay in their environ-
ment and associated it with corpses. "The realization of the possibility that
death may be total annihilation probably came very gradually . . . We do
not know when and how the association between death and decay origi-
nated. This association was, perhaps, a decisive factor leading to the conception of death as total destruction."[15]

Fast on the heels of the certainty of death, of human mortality, came
the fear of death that we see evidenced in the writings of the early literate
cultures. In *Gilgamesh*, for example, we find: "When I die, shall I not be
like unto Enkidu? Sorrow entered my heart, I am afraid of death."[16] In *The
Odyssey*, Achilles' shade tells Odysseus that he would rather be a slave in
the real world of the living than king of the dead. The dead are described
as living on without their wits as disembodied ghosts. They are, literally,

shades or shadows. In order to communicate with Odysseus they have to drink from the river of black blood. Odysseus says to the shade of Achilles that he must be a mighty prince among the dead, "For you, Achilles, Death should have lost his sting." But Achilles rebukes him: "Spare me your praise of Death. Put me on earth again, and I would rather be a serf in the house of some landless man, with little enough for himself to live on, than king of all these dead men that have done with life."[17] Hades, for Homer, was the habitat of shades. Wandering on the earth was the sentence of shades who were dismembered or eaten by dogs.

The Homeric vision of death is not unlike the one Ethan Edwards attributes to the Comanche. If your corpse is desecrated, you will wander forever between the winds and never make it to the spiritland. MacIntyre writes, "Death in Homer is an unmixed evil; the ultimate evil is death followed by desecration of the body."[18] It is clear from Homer that the early Greeks feared death, or certainly did not welcome it, because at best one would be reduced to a witless, disembodied shadow of one's living self. Plato's doctrine of the immortality of the soul and his descriptions of the afterlife in a number of his dialogues may have, in part, been intended as a response to the fear of death that the Homeric picture encouraged. Plato wrote, " 'But how shall we bury you?' 'Anyway you like,' replied Socrates, 'that is, if you can catch me and I don't slip through your fingers.' He laughed gently as he spoke, and turning to us went on, 'I can't persuade Crito, that I am this Socrates here who is talking to you now and marshaling all the arguments. He thinks that I am the one whom he will see presently lying dead, and he asks how he is to bury me! As for my long and elaborate explanation that when I have drunk the poison I shall remain with you no longer, but depart to a state of heavenly happiness, this attempt to console both you and myself seems to be wasted on him.' "[19]

The survival of death, for Plato, and later Descartes, depends on the conception of souls as substances capable of independent existence, totally incorporeal. Plato, as is well known, offers a number of arguments throughout his dialogues to support the identification of the soul with the person. Descartes tells us, "I know with certainty that I exist, and that I find that absolutely nothing else belongs necessarily to my nature or essence except that I am a thinking being, I readily conclude that my essence consists solely in being a body which thinks [or a substance whose whole essence or nature is to think]. And although perhaps, or rather certainly . . . I have a body with which I am very closely united, nevertheless, . . . it is certain that this 'I' [that is to say my soul, by virtue of which I am what I am-] is entirely [and truly] distinct from my body and that it can [be or] exist without it."[20]

Saint Paul, it will be recalled from earlier in the chapter, appears committed to the notion that a bodily form is needed to sustain human identity. On his account a celestial body will be fashioned by God, presumably in the image of the terrestrial person. Paul is confident that God will perform the second creation, thereby placing what David Lewis might call "counterparts"[21] of those who have died earthly deaths in another world and in that world those counterparts will be more like the earthly deceased than anything else in that world.[22]

To carry this image on a bit further into the Christian position, those counterparts in the "next world" will either eternally undergo tortures or bask in the glow of heaven. That is a long time to suffer for what someone else did! Of course, the tormented replica persons in Hell presumably would have memories of having done wicked things on Earth, but they cannot really remember doing those earthly deeds, because they were never earthly creatures. They are only surrogates for their earthly predecessors. They would not be the people even they honestly think they are.

As Saul Kripke[23] argues, in counterpart theory regret is incomprehensible. The counterfactual claim that nestles in such regret is not about me, for example, existing in some other world or in some possible situation. It is about my counterpart. A claim about me, someone who is entirely distinct from my counterpart, no matter how much my counterpart resembles me, cannot be the basis for my counterpart having regrets. Even if my celestial body's counterpart in this world is my terrestrial body (and the theory does not require that it is), that fact provides no basis for celestial regret. The Pauline Hell cannot be populated with anyone who genuinely regrets his earthly counterpart's terrestrial misdeeds.

Saint Thomas Aquinas wrote that "It is clear that man is not a soul only, but something composed of soul and body . . . If a man cannot be happy in this life, we must of necessity hold the resurrection. Souls are indestructible, immortal. But bodies clearly decay and decompose in death. We cannot call it resurrection unless the soul returns to the same body, since resurrection is a second rising, and the same thing rises that falls."[24] Surely Saint Thomas was not imagining a sequel to *The Night of the Living Dead*! He maintains that one's resurrection body will not be numerically identical with one's earthly body, but it will be qualitatively identical to it. One's soul retains the form of one's body, so one's resurrection body must, therefore, assume that form in the reconstitution process. Identity is preserved, or so we are supposed to be persuaded.

The fear of inevitable death for the Christian (and the preChristian/ postHomeric Greek) was, it would seem, in large measure relieved by any of these various conceptions of the person and the preservation of the person's identity, all of which respond positively to the hope that an individual's life is not annihilated in death or at best left as but a witless shade. Whether or not one should take solace in a nonannihilation (survivalist) theory has, of course, been a topic of discussion by philosophers since antiquity.

V

It is instructive for present purposes to examine the way death is still popularly portrayed, symbolized, in our culture, even now nearly into the twenty-first century, as Fred Feldman has noted.[25] The most familiar depiction is that of a hooded skeleton carrying a huge scythe: the Grim Reaper. The image is purposefully ugly, menacing, frightening. The Reaper's two most distinctive features, as Feldman notes, are that it is mysterious (its face is generally hidden in the shadows of the hood) and it is evil. The symbol conveys the point that, for us, death is the standard by which we measure all other misfortunes.

Whether or not you think that death is mysterious, you might find it hard to believe that it is not evil. Still, a number of philosophers have argued that there is nothing particularly evil about death. The most notable perhaps was Epicurus. He wrote to Menoeceus:

> Become accustomed to the belief that death is nothing to us. For all good and evil consists in sensation, but death is the deprivation of sensation. And therefore a right understanding that death is nothing to us makes the mortality of life enjoyable, not because it adds to it an infinite span of time, but because it takes away the craving for immortality. For there is nothing terrible in life for the man who truly comprehended that there is nothing terrible in not living. So that the man speaks but idly who says that he fears death not because it will be painful when it comes, but because it is painful in anticipation. For that which gives no trouble when it comes, is but an empty pain in anticipation. So death, the most terrifying of ills, is nothing to us, since so long as we exist death is not with us; but when death comes, then we do not exist. It does not then concern either the living or the dead, since for the former it is not, and the latter are no more.[26]

Epicurus was responding in his day to a growing fear of death as a time of pain and sorrow and to the complaint that the fear of death takes the joy out of living because it involves the knowledge that all of our most prized projects may be terminated before we can complete them. Some might have said that if you know you are going to die and that you will be annihilated in death, that living well is impossible. In other words, "What's the point?" A dark black cloud hangs always over your head. How can you enjoy the present when tomorrow you die and everything you have been working for no longer is your project? You have no more projects. Epicurus's response is to defend life by making less of death. "We will leave life crying aloud in a glorious triumph song that we have lived well," he writes. (His words—if they could have been read by the Christians of the Middle Ages, though they could not have been, even had his letter been available to them—might have given a wholly new direction to those Christians who were beset on all sides with a fascination with the horrors of death and the tortures of Hell. By the Middle Ages, the Pauline message of the joys of resurrection and of a postmortem life in a heavenly paradise had been de-emphasized in favor of all manner of depiction of the torments and sufferings of the damned.)

Lucretius followed Epicurus's lead when he wrote:

For thou shalt sleep, and never wake again,
And quitting life, shalt quit thy living pain . . .
The worst that can befall thee, measured right,
Is a sound slumber, and a long good-night . . .[27]

Epicurus and Lucretius are what I think we can fairly call Annihilators regarding human death. They do not deny or defy death. They accept it, but the terms of their acceptance are that it annihilates the human and so cannot be an evil to that person. What they mean is that insofar as being dead is not a painful experience for the deceased, it cannot be a bad thing for the deceased. If they are right, they believe, then not existing is not something anyone can rationally fear. Death is not an evil (or a good) for the dead. "Death is nothing to us."

The arguments of Epicurus and Lucretius go astray in at least one very important part. They rightly maintain that death is not painful for the dead, and being hedonists they identify only pain with what is intrinsically bad or evil. So, of course, death is not intrinsically bad for the one who is dead. He or she has no pain, no suffering, no sensations at all. But things can still be bad for someone even if they are not intrinsically bad for him or her, even in the hedonist's theory. The badness or evil of those things is derivative in that they happen to connect to pain in some way. They are extrinsically bad. Epicurus and Lucretius overlook the possibility, as Feldman does not, that death, though not intrinsically bad may well be extrinsically bad for the deceased.[28]

Suppose you ate a particularly tasty meal that you thoroughly enjoyed, but the meal was laced with a slow-acting poison that will make you very sick hours and hours after you ate the meal. The Epicurean would not say that eating the meal was intrinsically bad for you. You enjoyed it. But he or she will say that eating the meal was extrinsically bad for you. Surely, we can agree that if one feels no pain while dead, that death cannot be intrinsically bad for the deceased. Death is not bad in itself. But is it, therefore, also not extrinsically bad for the person who dies? Maybe death is like eating a very tasty meal that is laced with poison, not itself painful, but still extrinsically bad. In that case death would be bad for the dead because of what it indirectly does to the dead. But how could death be even extrinsically bad for the dead person when it cannot link up to anything that is intrinsically bad for the person? After all, the dead have no pains and so no intrinsically bad things happening to them. Nothing can cause them intrinsic bads, so there seems to be nothing for the extrinsic badness of death to lead to in the way of intrinsic badness for the deceased. The Epicurean point would be that insofar as death never involves intrinsic bads, it cannot also involve extrinsic bads for the dead. "You are just dead," as Chollo says in *Lonesome Dove*.

Feldman maintains that the Epicurean-like argument that depends on the causal connection between extrinsic and intrinsic bads is faulty. He defends the view that things can be extrinsically bad for someone in ways that do not depend on the extrinsic bad causing an intrinsic bad.[29] Consider a version of his example. Suppose you were accepted for admission by two colleges, A and B. You decided to go to A. You spent four happy and successful years getting a degree at A, but you never studied taxidermy because A had no courses in taxidermy. You never learned anything about taxidermy; yet, just suppose, you have a genuinely outstanding aptitude for taxidermy and you would have enjoyed studying it more than you enjoyed any subject you studied at A. College B offers a full series of courses in taxidermy. Suppose that you go to your grave never realizing how much enjoyment you missed. If you had gone to B, you would have become a taxidermist and your life would have been much happier than it was. Your lifelike creations, even reconstructed from roadkill, would have graced natural history museums around the world. I think we might be willing to say that attending A was actually bad for you, or unfortunate, or a pity because you would have been happier in life had you gone to B. Yet, though attending A was bad for you, it was not in itself a painful experience. It caused you no real pain. And because you never learned of your aptitude for taxidermy, you never felt any loss or sorrow at not having pursued that career. If the example is convincing, extrinsic badness need not link causally to intrinsic badness, at least in the way the hedonists define it, namely, as pain. In fact, the extrinsic badness does not link up with any pain at all in the example. There is no simple causal connection between the two types of badness. But there is a kind of link, a link related to how things would have been had something occurred that, in fact, did not occur.

From this, a principle emerges that I will call the Feldman principle: "Something is extrinsically bad for a person if and only if he or she would have been intrinsically better off if it had not taken place." So some things are extrinsically bad for us even though they cause no pain and do not lead to painful experiences. They are not intrinsically bad. But they deprive us of the intrinsic value we would have enjoyed had they not taken place. Death may be like that, at least for a great number of people. Its badness depends not on the pain it causes but on what would have taken place if it had not occurred when it did. Death, therefore can be bad without the need of Hell or causing pain and suffering.

Blue, Will Penny's fellow cowhand, says to Will in reference to their mutual friend Dutchy who is gut shot, "We been workin' the same outfits three, four, years runnin'. He's a good old boy. This ain't no good way for him to go, Will." To which Will sardonically replies, "Tell ya, Blue, ain't no good way to go."

Consider the following example (also borrowed from Feldman).[30] A young boy is undergoing a minor surgical procedure, a tonsillectomy. The administration of anesthesia is faulty and the boy dies while unconscious on the operating table. His death is painless. But surely his death is a misfortune for him. It might be fair to say that had he lived he would likely have had a full life in which, on the whole, he would have been happy. "This boy's life contains less intrinsic value for him, measured hedonistically, than it would have contained if he had not died when he did."[31] On the Feldman principle, the boy's "death is extrinsically bad for him even though it is not itself a painful experience, and it causes him no pain . . . Death is not a sort of pain."[32] He suffered no painful experience. And he is not suffering pain now while dead. He is not thinking about what might have been with his life, that it was intrinsically less valuable for him than it might have been had he not died when he did. He is not thinking. He is dead. As Feldman notes, "The evil of death is a matter of deprivation."[33] The deprivation is of what would have been an intrinsic good. Of course, this will only be the case when it makes sense to say that one would have been better off had one's death not occurred when it did.

With some people who are racked with pain incessantly, a continuation of their lives of suffering would be an intrinsic bad or evil for them and were they to die in their sleep, or perhaps end their lives in some painless fashion, death would not be extrinsically bad for them. In fact, it would be an extrinsic good.

On the view I have here adopted, the extrinsic goodness or badness of death is going to happen after the person in question is dead and therefore no longer in existence. Does that make any sense? I think it does. The crucial factor is the value of the life led by the person until the time when death occurs. It will either be lower or higher than the value of the life he or she would have led if death does not occur at that time. Simply, a person does not have to exist at the time when something extrinsically bad or good happens to him or her. Of course, a person has to exist for something intrinsically bad or good to happen to him or her. In working all of this out, the values in question relate to comparable possible lives: the life terminated at time t and the life terminated some time later, $t + 1$.

In *The Shootist*, Doc Hostetler lays out for J. B. Books, the gunfighter stricken with cancer, how his life will go if the cancer progresses, as it inevitably will.

> Hostetler: One morning you're just going to wake up and say 'Here I am in this bed and here I'm goin' to stay . . . The pain will become unbearable. If you're lucky, you'll lose consciousness. 'Til then you'll scream . . . There's one more thing I'd say. Both of us have had a lot to do with death. I'm not a brave man, but you must be. Now this is not advice. It's not even a suggestion. It's just something for you to reflect on while your mind's still clear.
> Books: What?
> Hostetler: I would not die a death like I just described.
> Books: No?
> Hostetler: Not if I had your courage.
> Books: Oh, thanks.

I will be discussing Books's courage in chapter 5. The point is that the doctor gives Books a look at two possible lives that he, Books, will live: the one he will live if the cancer progresses and the one that will end before the onset of the described extreme pain, if he commits suicide as the doctor seems to be suggesting. Books, as the film progresses, actually works out a third option. In any event, it is clear that a relatively quick and painless death in Books's case would not be extrinsically bad for him. Recall the burial scene in *The Cowboys*. In that case, Will Anderson pronounces that the deceased was a good boy and would have become a good man. The clear implication is that his was a bad death, that is, a death that was extrinsically bad for the boy. In *Will Penny*, both Blue and Will realize that the twenty-seven-year-old Dutchy's death will be a bad one for him. But, in

The Shootist Books is searching for a good death to culminate a life he is proud to have lived. The potential weeks of extreme suffering that the cancer promises to give him certainly fail to meet that description.

Remember, however, that the thrust of Epicurus's letter to Menoeceus was to relieve his correspondent of the fear of death. The point was that because there is no pain in being dead that one should not fear death. If that is what Menoeceus feared with respect to death, then he should have been placated by Epicurus's argument. No one should fear death because they believe it is a painful experience. Death is not an experience at all. Even the Christians don't think that death is an experience. For them, experiences come before and after death. Death is some sort of mysterious transportation or transformation. Suppose, however, that Menoeceus did not fear death because he thought it would be a painful experience. Suppose he believed, and according to Feldman he might be right in his own case, as each of us may be in ours, that if he dies he will be deprived of some pleasure, something of intrinsic value to him. If that is what he thought, then Epicurus entirely missed the target in trying to convince him that death was nothing. It is, clearly, something to him, and it is something bad.

VI

In all of this, where does the westerner fit? Westerners are Annihilators. They are certainly not Survivalists, like Plato and the Christians. But they are not at all in league with Epicurus, Lucretius, and their like. They ride with an altogether different posse of Annihilators. Death is not nothing; it is virtually everything to the westerner. And it is an evil to be rationally feared. That is because it is generally an extrinsic evil in that it deprives the westerner of what is of intrinsic value to him, what he most cares about, for example, his free life in the wilderness. It is everything, not because he has hope of surviving it, but because death culminates and annihilates his life. There is nothing important to a life after death (except perhaps for reputation, fond thoughts, and a reason for vengeance on the part of the living), and so how a person dies or rather how a person faces death and risks of death where he ought to be afraid is the key to the virtue of that person. The Western's conception of death is embedded an Homeric Greek ideal. C. M. Bowra writes of the classical Greek experience that "the exponents of the heroic ideal regard death as the climax and completion of life, the last and most searching ordeal to which a man is subjected and the true test of his worth."[34]

The westerner's view of death also echoes certain Old Testament conceptions. For example, in Ecclesiastes 9:10 we are told, "Whatsoever thy hand findeth to do, do it with thy might; for there is no work, nor device, nor knowledge, nor wisdom, in the grave whither thou goest." More important, however, the westerner views his conception of death as the foundation of true moral virtue and the immortality conceptions of the Survivalist Christian easterners as morally deficient. His conception is decidedly anti-Kantian.

Kant held that an eternal afterlife is essential to the highest achievement of moral virtue, and that we are required by moral law to accomplish such an end. He wrote: "The achievement of the highest good (*summum bonum*) in the world is the necessary object of a will determinable by moral law. In such a will, however, the complete fitness of intentions to the moral law is the supreme condition of the highest good. This aptness, therefore, must be just as possible as its object, because it is contained in the command that requires us to promote the latter."[35] This was, I suppose, Kant's version of that admonition in the Sermon on the Mount to "be ye perfect even as your Father in Heaven is perfect," that triggered Pelagius's ruminations on the earthly perfectibility of humans. In any event, Kant sees in this moral requirement the foundation of his "argument" for eternal life. "Thus the Highest Good is practically possible only on the supposition of the immortality of the soul, and the latter, as inseparably bound to the moral law, is a postulate of pure practical reason."[36] Such a postulate, for Kant, is not really capable of demonstration or proof, but must, nonetheless, be taken to be the case because it cannot be separated from—it is "an inseparable corollary of"—some practical law that he believes he has shown to be "unconditionally valid." The idea is that progress toward perfectibility is a basic moral requirement, something we morally ought to do, and "ought" implies "can." Although we cannot achieve perfectibility—the highest good—in our lives on earth, if we live eternal lives, we would be able to make continual progress toward fulfilling the moral requirement. In short, the fact that perfectibility is a moral obligation entails that we must be immortal or we should never be able to meet the obligation, and if we cannot meet it, it cannot be a moral obligation. But it is a moral obligation, so . . .

The westerner would probably find himself in sympathy with the sentiments of Pietro Pomponazzi, who wrote, "Those who maintain the mortality of the soul can be shown to save the essence and reason of virtue better than those who believe the soul immortal."[37] Pomponazzi's idea was that the hope of eternal reward and the fear of eternal punishment create weak, servile humans whose behavior is not genuinely governed by true virtue, but only by a virtue impressed on them under duress. Insofar as we usually would not credit someone for acts, even good acts, done under duress, under threat, we should not regard as virtuous those whose virtue is linked to immortality. Michel de Montaigne added, "I find nothing so lowly and mortal in the life of Alexander as his fancies about becoming immortal."[38] Time and again in the films, westerners echo these sentiments and they hold themselves apart from those whose sense of ethics are dependent on the promise of survival of death and eternal life.

In large measure, the westerner's outlook toward life and death reflects the autobiographic "trials," the *essai*, of Montaigne when he wrestles with his own understanding of death and ethics. In book 3 of his *Essays*, Montaigne writes:

> If you do not know how to die, never mind. Nature will give you full and adequate instruction on the spot . . . We trouble our life by thoughts about death, and our death by thoughts about life. The first saddens us, the second terrifies us . . . A quarter of an hour's suffering, without any hurtful consequences, does not deserve special lessons . . . If we have not known how to live, it is wrong to teach us how to die, and to give the end a different shape from the whole . . . It seems to me that death is indeed the end but not the aim of life; it is the conclusion, its extreme point, yet not its object. Life should contain its own aim, its own purposes . . . Among the many duties included under the general and principal head of knowing how to live, is this article of knowing how to die . . .[39]

Montaigne is railing against the fascination in his time with the *ars moriendi* schooling in easy death, but what he says about death and living is virtually repeated by Robert Ryan's character in *The Naked Spur*. "Choosin' the way to die makes no difference . . . Choosin' how to live. That's the hard part."

The westerner's distaste for those who waste their lives on foolish things, who let their lives slip past, who worry more about the future than making something of the present is distinctly Montaignean, and, because so much of Montaigne's reflections are derived, and often quoted, from Seneca, there might seem to be Roman Stoic character in it as well. Montaigne writes, "I am resigned to lose my life without regret, but as something whose nature it is to be lost, not as a troublesome burden. Moreover, not to dislike the idea of dying is truly possible only in one who enjoys living. It needs great management to enjoy life . . . When I feel mine to be so brief in time, I am anxious to increase it in weight . . . The shorter my possession of life the deeper and fuller I must make it."[40] Later on he adds: "The man who knows how to enjoy his existence as he ought has attained

The typical women of the western: The prostitute, Dallas, and the good Christian woman, Lucy Mallory, at the stage way-station. *Stagecoach. Courtesy of the Museum of Modern Art, New York, New York.*

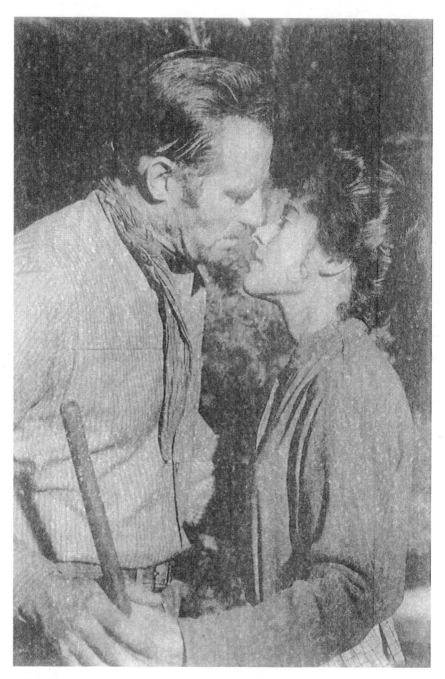

Will and Catherine. *Will Penny.*

Garth meets Tess Millay. *Red River.*

J.B. Books gives Gillom Rogers a lesson in shooting and moral codes. *The Shootist.*

Courtesy of the Museum of Modern Art, New York, New York.

"I don't hold jail against you, but I hate a liar."

"Well, you're a hard man, Mr. Anderson."

"Well, it's a hard life." *The Cowboys.*

Courtesy of the Museum of Modern Art, New York, New York.

After a night together, the hotel owner's wife expresses concern for the stranger's safety. *High Plains Drifter.*

Courtesy of the Museum of Modern Art, New York, New York.

Megan and her savior: the Preacher (Death). *Pale Rider.*
Courtesy of the Museum of Modern Art, New York, New York.

Tom Dunson surveys his cattle herd after burying a Mexican he shot.
"The Lord giveth and the Lord taketh away." *Red River.*

Courtesy of the Museum of Modern Art, New York, New York.

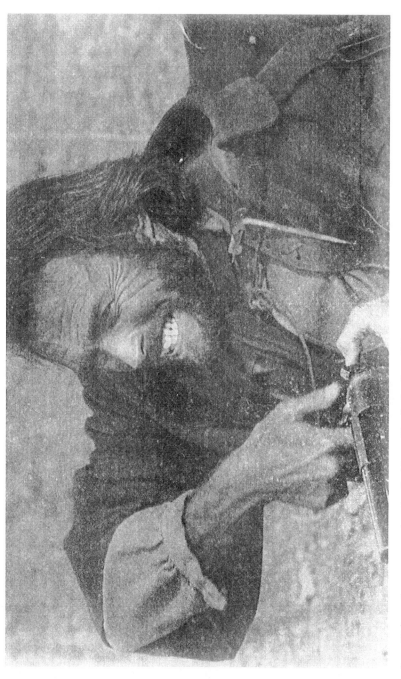

Josey Wales seeks revenge against the Red Legs. *The Outlaw Josey Wales.*
Courtesy of the Museum of Modern Art, New York, New York.

Cable Hogue spends his final moments with Hildy, Joshua, and Bowen. *The Ballad of Cable Hogue.*

Courtesy of the Museum of Modern Art, New York, New York.

Shane uses the butt of his gun to end his fight with Joe Starrett over who will face the
Rikers and Wilson. *Shane.*

Courtesy of the Museum of Modern Art, New York, New York.

Ransom Stoddard meets Liberty Valance in the showdown on the streets of Shinbone. *The Man Who Shot Liberty Valance.*

Courtesy of the Museum of Modern Art, New York, New York.

to an absolute perfection, like that of the gods. We seek other conditions because we do not understand the proper use of our own, and go out of ourselves because we do not know what is within us. So it is no good our mounting on stilts, for even on stilts we have to walk with our own legs; and upon the most exalted throne in the world it is still our own bottom that we sit on."[41]

Such sentiments are expressed over and over again in Westerns by the true westerners, both heroes and villains. For examples look in *The Big Country* at the way Rufus Hannassey addresses Henry Terrell at the party at Terrell's ranch; in *The Ox-Bow Incident* at the way Major Tetley is viewed by the townspeople after the lynching, in *The Tall T* at the treatment of Willard Mims, the bookkeeper, by both Randolph Scott's Patrick and Richard Boone's Frank; in *Stagecoach* at the responses to Mr. Gatewood, the banker, in *Hombre* at the way Russell and the other passengers deal with Dr. Favor; in *Once Upon a Time in the West* at the way both Cheyenne and the villain Frank react to the railroad baron Morton, whom Cheyenne calls "Mr. Choo Choo"; in *The Ballad of Cable Hogue* at the good-natured, but pointed, way Cable Hogue treats Quinter, the stagecoach owner; and in *High Plains Drifter* at the way all of the prominent residents of Lago are dealt with by Clint Eastwood's character.

Montaigne's point, and one with which the westerner would concur, is that the temporality of life constitutes its most important feature. Montaigne quips, "You do not die because you are sick, you die because you are alive."[42] One of the reasons the westerner says so little and detests the talkative easterner is that talk is life-wasting. Time is of the essence and not to be talked away. The Christians (the easterners in the films) act as though the temporality of life were of no special consequence; in fact, they deny that characteristic in favor of staking a claim on eternal life. In doing so, they devalue life and living, and that is to diminish their own value as persons.

Life does not gain value in its extension.[43] The value of a life is in what the person has done with his or her time, no matter how long, no matter how short. This idea in Montaigne, expressed as "The shorter my possession of life the deeper and fuller I must make it," is, however, not a stoic sentiment. Montaigne leaves behind Seneca and the other stoics. He is not expressing resignation to the fates of life and eventual annihilating death. He is preaching the gospel of the Renaissance, an "appreciation of the exciting and wonderful world surrounding man, and the new feeling that life can be pleasant and must be enjoyed . . . One's life must not be tolerated and suffered, but can be changed, can be molded, according to one's freely chosen plan, can and should be lived more intensely and vigorously, so that one is almost tempted to see in Montaigne's position the first anticipation of Nietzsche's appeal to 'live dangerously'."[44]

In no small measure the heroes of Western films fulfill Montaigne's ideals. Recall Vallian's "My life ain't that bad, ma'am. To me, it's the best, always the best." The westerner rides in the shadow of death and he fears the evil of a premature death, not an afterlife, because such a death will cost him intrinsic goods. And he knows that, when he kills another person, he has deprived him of such goods. In *Unforgiven* William Munny explains killing to the Schofield Kid, "It's a hell of a thing to kill a man. You take away everything he's got . . . and everything he's ever going to have." He accepts the temporality of human life and recognizes exactly that as the value of human life. Because it is short, it matters. Learning to live it fully, even dangerously, and well is the primary lesson he has learned and teaches as he rides west. That is the central point of the Louis L'Amour tale of the MacAskills and Conn Vallian (*The Quick and the Dead*; and also of his *Conagher*. It is the theme of such coming of age Westerns as *Red River* and *The Cowboys*, and it plays no small part in *Lonesome Dove*. In the end, it is also the lesson that the Preacher gives Megan, the answer to her prayer in *Pale Rider*, another coming of age Western.

The Western, however, tells more of the story, and it is a rather sad one. The westerner inevitably is being driven into a smaller and smaller wilderness by the gardening easterner. Civilization destroys his habitat. Life's value in the living is being converted to a meaning in the after-dying. The renaissance is being unceremoniously ushered into middle-aged capitalistic Christianity. Megan prays, "I'd like to get more of this life first!" and then, as she looks up to the snow-covered mountains, "Just one miracle." Her miracle arrives, and he is Death, the Pale Rider, and he does bring her more of this life, or rather the understanding that death makes this life worth living well, that an ethics based in an annihilation conception of death may be more vigorous, more life-affirming, than one dependent on the immortality of the soul or the resurrection of the body, and an everlasting life after death.

Always facing death as an annihilation of yourself and still making something out of your life, whatever its span, is the moral imperative of the westerner. Death ends your life, and your life project, whenever it is "your turn." That is it. You will never get another chance and never get to continue after death. Wittgenstein wrote in the *Tractatus* (6.4311): "Death is not an event in life: We do not live to experience death." and (6.431) "So too at death the world does not alter, but comes to an end."[45] When the westerner sums up a life at those awkward burials on the prairie, he is saying all that matters and all that there is:

In *Cowboy*: "All we know is that a man is dead and that's that . . . He was a good man with cattle. He always did the best he knew how. I hope somebody can say the same over me."

In *The Cowboys*: "This was a good boy. He'd a been a good man. But he didn't get the chance. Death can come for you anyplace, anytime. It's never welcome, but if you've done all you can do and it's your best, in a way, I guess, you're ready for him."

In *The Outlaw Josey Wales*: ". . . never turned his back on his folks or his kind. I rode with him; I got no complaints."

In *Lonesome Dove*: ". . . served with me thirty years, fought in twenty-one engagements with the Comanche and the Kiowa, cheerful in all weathers, never shirked a task. Splendid behavior."

Tompkins writes, "Once you no longer believe you are eternal spirit, risking your life becomes the supreme form of heroism, the bravest thing a person can do."[46] She is only partly right in her characterization. Insofar as risking your life is what you do all the time you are alive, it is not necessarily an act of heroism to risk your life. Heroism, even for one who does not believe he is an eternal spirit, requires more than mere life-risking. Tompkins conflates heroism with extreme risk-taking. There is more to it than that, and I will try to explain what more is involved in chapter 5. On her account, villains as well as heroes would be heroic in Westerns. They may both be tough, but there is an important moral difference between them as they risk their lives in the face of immanent annihilation.

Notes

1. Corinthians, 15.

2. Ibid., 15: 22–55.

3. Gilbert Murray, *Stoic, Christian and Humanist* (London, 1940), 32.

4. Jacques Choron, *Death and Western Thought* (New York, 1963), chap. 8.

5. Ibid., quoted on p. 86.

6. See Peter French, "The Survival of My Counterpart," *Southern Journal of Philosophy*, 20, No. 1 (1982): 53–60.

7. Tompkins, *West of Everything*, 36.

8. See Peter French, *Responsibility Matters* (Lawrence, KS, 1992), chap. 3.

9. Michael Kearl, *Endings* (New York, 1989), 32. I learned a great deal about the sociology of death not only from Mike's book, but from many stimulating conversations with him when we were colleagues at Trinity University. The distinctions between death-defying, death-denying, and death-accepting is, in part, owed to Mike.

10. Ibid., 37.

11. Alan Harrington, *The Immortalist* (Millbrae, CA, 1977), 1.

12. Choron, *Death and Western Thought*, 14.

13. Ibid.

14. Genesis, 3: 22–23. To whom is the Lord God speaking? What were such trees doing in the Garden in the first place?

15. Choron, *Death and Western Thought*, 25.

16. Alexander Heidel, trans., *The Gilgamesh Epic and the Old Testament Parallels* (Chicago, 1946), 64.

17. Homer, *The Odyssey*, translated by E. V. Rieu (New York, 1950), 156.

18. Alasdair MacIntyre, *After Virtue* (Notre Dame, Ind., 1984), 127.

19. Plato, *The Phaedo*, trans. Hugh Tredennick in *The Collected Dialogues of Plato*, ed. Hamilton and Cairns (Princeton, N.J., 1961), 95.

20. Rene Descartes, *Discourse on Method and Meditations*, trans. Laurence Lafleur (Indianapolis, Ind., 1960), 132.

21. See David Lewis, "Counterparts of Persons and Their Bodies," *Journal of Philosophy*, 68 (1971): 203–11.

22. On Lewis's account, individuals are worldbound, but an individual can have counterparts in possible worlds. Sentences about what someone might have done are understood to be about what a counterpart of that individual in the actual world does in some possible world. In his list of postulates of the theory (in English) Lewis includes the following: P1: Nothing is in anything except a world; P2: Nothing is in two worlds; P3: Whatever is a counterpart is in a world; P4: Whatever has a counterpart is in a world; P5: Nothing is a counterpart of anything else in its world; P6: Anything in a world is a counterpart of itself. Individuation of things within a world is no more a problem than it is in the actual world. The transworld identity problem is removed by P1 and P2.

Lewis explains the relationship between an individual and his counterparts as constituted on resemblances. Someone's counterparts resemble him closely in content and context and they are such that they resemble him or her more closely than any other thing in the worlds in which they exist. But they are not really that person. The key notion for Lewis is that of "close resemblance," which Lewis explicates by telling us that one's counterparts share his or her essential properties, but those properties need not be essential to the counterparts. Lewis suggests that being corporeal and being human may be among my essential attributes. If they are, then my counterpart must be corporeal and human. If afterlife is understood as the life of a counterpart, it will need to be a corporeal life. Hence, Pauline materialism could be consistent with counterpart theory. See David Lewis, "Counterpart Theory and Quantified Modal Logic," *Journal of Philosophy*, 65 (1968).

23. Saul Kripke, "Identity and Necessity," in *Identity and Individuation*, ed. M. Munitz (New York, 1971), 148–49.

24. St. Thomas Aquinas, *Summa Theologica,* trans. the Fathers of the English Dominican Province (London, 1912), pt. 3, questions 69–86, "Of the Resurrection."

25. Fred Feldman, *Confrontations With The Reaper* (New York, 1992), 3.

26. Epicurus, *Letter to Menoeceus*, trans. C. Bailey in *The Stoic and Epicurean Philosophers*, ed. W. J. Oates (New York, 1940), 30–34.

27. Lucretius, *De Rerum Natura*, trans. H. A. J. Munro in *The Stoic and Epicurean Philosophers*.

28. See Feldman, *Confrontations With The Reaper*, chap. 8.

29. Ibid., 138–42.

30. Ibid., 139.

31. Ibid.

32. Ibid.

33. Ibid.

34. C. W. Bowra, *The Greek Experience* (New York, 1959), 49.

35. Immanuel Kant, *Critique of Practical Reason,* (1788), trans. L. W. Beck (Chicago, 1949), 225.

36. Ibid., 226.

37. Pietro Pomponazzi, "On the Immortality of Man," in *The Renaissance Philosophy of Man* (Chicago, 1950), 375.

38. Michel de Montaigne, *Essays*, trans. J. M. Cohen (New York, 1958), 406.

39. Ibid., 329.

40. Ibid., 401.

41. Ibid., 406.

42. Ibid., 376–77.

43. A point made in the play *The Makropolous Case* by Karel Capek.

44. Choron, *Death and Western Thought*, 101.

45. Ludwig Wittgenstein, *Tractatus Logico Philosophicus*, trans. D. F. Pears and B. F. McGuinness (London, 1961), 147.

46. Tompkins, *West of Everything*, 31.

· 4 ·

TRAGEDY, GRACE, AND PRIDE

I

With so much emphasis on death, especially sudden death, one might reasonably expect Westerns to be depressing, sad films. By and large, they are not. They celebrate life and bring to it a meaning that is only possible when death is squarely faced, accorded its due, as life's climax, and even as a potential vindicating and authenticating moment. We can agree with Tompkins that Westerns, though death-oriented, death-accepting, and death-focused, are not tragedies.[1] At least, they are not tragedies in the way tragedy usually has been characterized in literary analyses throughout the centuries. The heroes of Westerns do not fit the standard molds of tragic heroes, though sometimes they come close. Some of the villains, however, very nearly personify the traditional tragic ideal.

Tragedy, of course, comes in many forms. The Greek tragedy, as Aristotle[2] and W. H. Auden[3] characterized it, was the tragedy of inevitability. Due to a basic flaw in the character of the protagonist, usually identified with ignorance masked by hubris, the unhappy fate of an admirable character is sealed. There is no way events can be prevented from spinning out in the way they do from the wheel of fate. "The *hubris* which is the flaw in the Greek hero's character is the illusion of a man who knows himself strong and believes that nothing can shake that strength."[4] Something, of course, does shake it, and he is tumbled from his comfortable position. The westerner, whether as hero or villain, shares with the Greek tragic hero a knowledge of his strengths; but, though confident in himself, he is far less convinced of his invincibility. Perhaps one major difference between the hero and the villain in the Western is that the hero sustains himself with a quiet confidence in his strengths, while the villain is prone to boasting. Still, neither is given much to words, and both let their skills "do the talkin."

The typical story line of the Western conveys a sense of inevitability. The "good guy" and the "bad guy" must eventually meet, and neither can walk away from the confrontation. The hero (as well as the villain) intuits this inevitability. There is a marvelous moment in *The Tall T* in which Randolph Scott's character, Patrick, lets the villain, played by Richard Boone, ride off. Boone rides a way up into the mountains, then turns his horse and gallops back to have it out with Scott, who is waiting for him, knowing that Boone cannot ride away from their confrontation. One of them must die there, face to face. And, of course, we know which one that will be. The hero must prevail, even though doing so drives an unremovable wedge between him and the community in whose name he has risked life and limb.

The sunset into which the hero will ride (or slowly amble) is not a shining good place where the hero can enjoy the fruits of his labors and the company of good people. It is a cold and lonely place where, we may be fairly assured, the sort of events that we have just seen unfold will reoccur, and death will always be a bullet away. In *The Searchers*, a movie filled with memorable scenes and indelibly marked moments, perhaps none is more vivid than its final scene. Even against his own obsessive will to both wreak vengeance on the Comanche chief Scar and kill his niece Debbie, who has become a Comanche squaw in his eyes, Ethan Edwards has rebuilt a family in the Texas wilderness by bringing Debbie to the Jorgensen's and uniting Martin and their daughter Laurie. The door of the Jorgensen's home is open to receive the new family. Ethan stands in the doorway for a moment or two. Then he turns away from the home and from us, the audience, and slowly ambles off to "wander forever between the winds."

There is another notable point concerning Ethan that touches on the tragic in *The Searchers*. It is that Ethan, though having dedicated five years of his life to the search for Debbie and Scar, does not gain the satisfaction of killing either. The killing of Scar is done awkwardly by the half-breed Martin in defense of Debbie and himself. It is not an act of vengeance for the horrific killings of Martha, Aaron, and Lucy as Ethan had intended. The whole epic of vengeance cycles into an act of self-defense, hardly what Ethan had planned. Deprived of the opportunity to kill Scar, Ethan viciously scalps the dead war chief and emerges from the teepee with the same sort of crazed look he had when he discovered the body of Martha after the Comanche's murder raid at the beginning of the film. That brutal act of mutilation, of scarring Scar, is all that Ethan is allowed, but at least it seems to be enough to soften his heart to Debbie. He decides not to kill her. But, at the end of the restoration, he is left savage, uncivilized, and unadmitted to the new family. In many ways, he is still the tortured man who rode in unexpectedly across Monument Valley and was seen by his lost love Martha through a door open to a family he could never join.

Aristotle, famously, told us that the perfect hero of a tragedy should be "a man though not outstandingly virtuous and just, [who] yet falls into misfortune not through vice or depravity but through some 'tragic flaw' "[5] Certainly, the westerner heroes are not preeminently virtuous and just, but, by and large, their misfortunes are not caused by some tragic flaw or personal fault. The values of the westerner and his lifestyle are, typically, totally vindicated, even if he personally is not. Furthermore, the westerner may display flaws of character that usually drive the plot; for example, Tom Dunson and Will Anderson are tyrannical, Josey Wales is obsessive, etc., but those flaws do not cause their eventual downfall and are usually overcome in external struggles and acts of vengeful violence. Though they cause suffering, both for the hero and others, their faults do not result in the hero's tragic downfall.

The westerners who become the villains of the stories, as suggested earlier, fit the Greek tragic picture rather better than the heroes. Sometimes, of course, the villains are mere one-dimensional caricatures, but in the better films they are fleshed out as having been hard-working, decent people who moved West and carved their fortunes and their empires from the unforgiving wilderness. In films like *Shane*, *The Missouri Breaks*, and *Pale Rider*, it is not strange to ask the sort of questions about the villains that many of us might be tempted to ask with respect to the fate of Oedipus: "When did he go wrong? What was the wrong choice he made that he should be brought to this end?" These types of villains seem to be caught in what Auden calls "the tragedy . . . that what had to happen happened."[6] It is almost senseless to ask why such a terrible end should befall the Rikers or LaHood or Braxton. Braxton, for example, in the opening scenes of *The Missouri Breaks*, explains to a horse thief he is about to hang that in the first year he came to Montana he turned the scrub-filled wilderness into pasture and in the second year he brought in eight thousand head of Texas cattle and thirty-five hundred volumes for his personal library. He prospered where no one else would even try, which naturally led him to adopt an authoritarian approach to anyone who would attempt to wrest his domain from him. It seems that the very characters of such villains, like that of Oedipus, require their fates as punishment for their audacity in being the sort of persons they are—persons who would and could create empires where others could not even survive.

It might be claimed that the Western, when it deals with such risk-taking entrepreneurs, is anticapitalistic. Though that may be true, the fuller picture is that the Western's villains, at least some of them, personify Greek tragic elements. Those Westerns, including *Shane*, *The Missouri Breaks*, and *Pale Rider*, embody something of the Greek pessimism that infests the tragedies of Sophocles: "an exceptional individual . . . must be guilty of hubris and be punished by a tragic fate."[7] As Auden notes, the chorus is the only alternative, and that role and that of the protagonist in the Greek tragedy are not self-selected. You can be exceptional and flawed and therefore doomed, or you can be average and weak and scrape by. Those are the only options. The homesteaders and the independent miners (and in some Westerns, the townspeople) are chorus.

I admit to feeling genuine pity for the likes of the Rikers, as well as Henry Terrell and his nemesis Rufus Hannassey in *The Big Country*, because their fates are sealed. To be where they are in the scheme of things, they have to have the sort of character flaws for which their downfalls are the only appropriate punishment. In other words, like the Greek tragic hero, their tragic situation is not caused directly by their character flaw. They are not punished for some specific thing they did due to their flaw. Their downfalls are ordained as punishment for their having that flaw in the first place. Still, they would not be who they are and in the positions they occupy had that flaw not been an integral part of their characters. We are led in the films to fault them for their stubbornness, their unwillingness to change their ways in the face of changing times, particularly for their refusal to share their land with the invading easterners. They are almost always shown to have huge tracts of land that are portrayed as underused. Their primary sin, it might appear, is a failure to abide by the Lockean Proviso, that there be "enough, and as good left in common for others."[8] Robert Nozick formulates the Proviso to give it a somewhat different focus, though one that does not exclude the matter of waste. He writes, "A process normally giving rise to a permanent bequeathable property right in a previously unowned thing will not do so if the position of others no longer at liberty to use the thing is thereby worsened."[9] It is, of course, not clear whether the cattle baron's acquisition of the valley does actually put the homesteaders in a worse position than they were before he acquired the land. After all, as the films make clear, at the time of acquisition the homesteaders were nowhere to be found in the West. They were still back East. They pulled up stakes and rode West to the cattle baron's valley uninvited. When they get there and discover the rancher is in possession, it is hard to see how they have been made worse off by the cattle baron's acquisition. They do not seem to have been driven below, in Nozick's terms, the baseline that could be set for them at the time of the rancher's acquisition. Cattle barons, in the films, typically make such an argument to the settlers, and they generally add that they made the land theirs by the sweat of their bodies, a solid Lockean claim to property. In response to the issue of waste, they explain that cattle ranching requires the vast acreage they have amassed.

This is something of an anticapitalistic spirit in the Western. The villains will not share the wealth, the natural resources, with the Johnny-Come-Latelys. And they wonder, sometimes quite persuasively, why they should share. Whether this anticapitalistic bent in the Western is also anti-American is an issue I prefer not to confront. In any event, the fall of the villain in these types of Westerns may well be something Sophocles and his contemporaries could have appreciated. What they could not have understood was why the focus of the plots almost always is on the plight of the chorus types or on the westerner hero, rather than the tragic figure from which, they might have thought, we could have much to learn.

II

Many of the westerner heroes, in the course of the plot, temporarily lose sight of who or what they really are. That might be identified as a version of a Greek tragic fault, a failure to "know thyself." No matter what they would like to think or hope, Shane never will be a homesteader and William Munny, Clint Eastwood's character in *Unforgiven*, will not ever be a successful pig farmer. Will Penny, though tempted by Catherine to become a farmer, recognizes that he cannot. Tom Logan, Jack Nicholson's character in *The Missouri Breaks*, may ultimately become a farmer, but he will not desert his outlaw crew, and he will take revenge on their cold-blooded killer, the regulator, played by Marlon Brando, and on Braxton as well. His violent acts are hardly those of a farmer, and, after he does them, he must desert his budding attempt at farming and "light out" for parts unknown, or at least unspecified, probably further West.

Though the hero's epistemic failures often provide a motivation for his involvement in death-risking situations, they are never fatal flaws in anything like the Greek sense. The hero's failures of self-knowledge are rectified in external actions, usually a gunfight or some other violent confrontation. And even if wounded, the hero wins. But does he? Homer in the last book of the *Iliad* teaches us something about winning in such confrontations that the westerner hero also not only has learned but surely accepts. The showdown, the gunfight, is not unlike the Greek confrontation of great warriors, the *agon*.

Combative contests fill the Homeric epic. One great warrior is described as meeting another in moral combat. One will win, one will lose. Each knows the other, at least by reputation. This goes on through the various books of the *Iliad*, but always looming in the background is the potential for that one great contest, the confrontation between the best of the Greeks and the best of the Trojans, between Achilles and Hector. Finally, after all of the obstacles to their match are removed, they take the field against one another. The combat, however, does not measure up to the hype. Hector tries to run away and three times desperately circles the city. He is unable to escape Achilles, and finally turns and fights. "Achilles saw that Hector's body was completely covered by the fine bronze armor he had taken from the great Patroclus when he killed him, except for an opening at the gullet where the collar bones lead over from the shoulders to the neck, the easiest place to kill a man. As Hector charged him, Prince Achilles drove at this spot with his lance; and the point went right through the tender flesh of Hector's neck, though the heavy bronze head did not cut his windpipe, and left him able to address his conqueror. Hector came down in the dust and the great Achilles triumphed over him."[10] Achilles then strips and desecrates Hector's body. He is clearly the winner. But when he later recants his decision to serve Hector's corpse to the dogs and gives it to Priam who is seeking the return of his son's body, we see that the very conception of the agon has changed. Winners are not purely and simply winners. To win may also be to lose. MacIntyre writes, "In the *Iliad* the character of these contests is gradually transformed until it is acknowledged in the confrontation between Achilles and Priam that to win is also to lose and that in the face of death winning and losing no longer divide."[11] The winning, when the contest is mortal, may radically differ from winning in, for example, basketball. When the Chicago Bulls win, they win. Homer tells us of Achilles, "He tossed to one side and the other . . . As memories crowded in on him, the warm tears poured down his cheeks. Sometimes he lay on his side, sometimes on his back, and then again on his face. At last he would get up and wander aimlessly along the salt sea beach."[12]

The westerner hero typically finds himself in a position not unlike that of Achilles. He wins, but he cannot enjoy the fruits of victory. He must leave the valley, the town, the community he has saved. They will not have him, and he, by and large, cannot have them. Such is the fate of Shane, Harmonica, Will Kane, and a number of others.

III

The Christians brought to tragedy the notion of salvation, which Auden believes converted the tragedy of inevitability into the tragedy of possibility, or rather, the tragedy of lost or squandered possibilities. Auden writes: "Christian tragedy is the tragedy of possibility, 'What a pity it was this way when it might have been otherwise.' . . . The Christian sin of pride is the illusion of a man who knows himself weak but believes he can by his own efforts transcend that weakness and become strong."[13]

Hamlet, for example, wastes his opportunities for the justified retribution of the death of his father because a certain kind of pride renders him unable to act at the propitious moment. He decides not to kill Claudius when Claudius appears to be praying because Claudius may therefore go to Heaven rather than where Hamlet wants to send him. In the Christian conception of things, the choice of Claudius's afterlife location, of course, is not Hamlet's, but God's. Hamlet's pride in thinking he has the right to make such a decision is subsequently made all the more ironic when we learn from Claudius that no matter how hard he tries, he cannot seem to pray. A westerner would just kill the usurper and be quick about it. "He needed killing!"

Captain Ahab, in *Moby Dick*, Auden's paradigm case of the Christian tragic hero, also squanders his salvation opportunities at a number of junctures in the novel. "A whale has bitten off his leg. What to the Greeks could only have been a punishment for sin is here a temptation to sin, an opportunity to choose; by making the wrong choice and continuing to make it, Ahab punishes himself."[14] Temptation, in the Christian tragic world view, is the confrontation with possibility. And among those possibilities that a person could choose is redemption. At least redemption; salvation is possible up to a point. In Ahab's case, that point is passed and he seals his fate, his damnation, on Auden's account, when he refuses to aid the *Rachel* in the search for its captain's lost boy, preferring instead to hunt the white whale and exact retribution on it for the horrible maiming it had done to him on a previous voyage.

Redemption is a powerful plot device in Christian and post-Christian drama. It dominates what the Christian cares about. But it can also show itself in Westerns. Steve Judd, the aging former lawman in *Ride the High Country*, tells Gil, his former partner with whom he is again joined for a final mission of transporting gold, "All I want is to enter my house justified." It is important, however, that Judd cares about entering "his house," not the House of the Lord, justified. What he wants is to die with a clear conscience, with the sense that he has done the right thing, despite the temptations to do otherwise that are laid in his path by Gil. His sense of redemption is crucially different from that presented to the hero in the Christian tragedy. The latter involves salvation, the former justification. Ultimately, I suspect, the Christian's life is never justified, but it can be saved. The opposite is the case for the westerner. He seeks to be justified in his death, but he has no hope or care for salvation.

The appealing quality of the westerner to me is that he is not saved or redeemed when he performs violent acts of punishment. Though civilization, which he detests, is typically saved (in another sense of the term), that is, made possible by his deeds, he remains unforgiven and quite literally, a dying breed. Ethan Edwards, Shane, the Preacher, William Munny, Link Jones (Gary Cooper's character in *Man of the West*) may enter their houses, their deaths, justified, but they will not be saved. Some of them, of course, will just keep riding West.

The Western, unlike the Christian tragedy, does not offer its characters the possibility of sainthood, a possibility that Christian tragic heroes by their choices can, and do, reject. Again, the contrast in world views is evident. The Western resists the imposition of the Christian framework to make sense of its confrontations with death. To gain the Christian possibility of sainthood, according to Auden, a person must of his or her free will surrender his or her will to the will of God, despite continual temptations to follow the dictates of his or her own desires. Westerners do not refuse the call of God. They never hear such a call because there is no God calling. Occasionally, however, there are comic ministers of the gospel to bellow what the westerner regards as the hollow message of Christianity. For example, in *The Ballad of Cable Hogue* the preacher, Joshua Sloan, arrives at the desert water hole that was discovered by Cable. Hogue stops him from taking a drink.

> Cable: Well, you're a sorry preacher and a hell of a sneak.
> Joshua: In my case those thus attributed often go hand in hand. . . . You are but a poor sinner in need of redemption. I will redeem you.
> Cable: Ten cents you pious bastard or I'll bury you. . . . What church did you say you was with, stranger?
> Joshua: The Church of the Wayfaring Stranger, a church of my own revelation.
> Cable: Just like that?
> Joshua: Just like that.
> Cable: Where's it located?
> Joshua: Wherever I go, it goes with me. . . .
> Cable(sarcastically): What a blessing religion must be, preacher. It touches my heart.

Westerners do get tempted, but it is usually by easterner women whose temptations, though sexual, also are bound with the taking up of tasks for which westerners are ill-suited: farming, shopkeeping, and the like. Remember Will Penny and Catherine Adams. Sometimes westerners give those tasks a try. But events draw them inextricably back to the way of the gun, to violence and vengeance, or they are killed when their pasts intrude on their new lives. In *Monte Walsh*, Chet Rollins, played by Jack Palance, is converted from a cowboy to a shopkeeper, but he is then senselessly killed in a robbery.

IV

There is something of what Tompkins calls a "sacramental aura"[15] about the westerner's confrontation with death, a sacrament with the religious drained from it. Where Ahab has the Christian God to confront, a God that is never far from the nineteenth century New England consciousness that pervades *Moby Dick*, the westerner confronts self-annihilation with no personal reckoning other than that which occurs in his own mind at the death-risking moment. The long, almost interminable, close-ups of main characters in shoot-outs are not presented as confessional preparations, laden with hopes of forgiveness, before meeting one's maker. They provide us with a look into the consciousness of someone who recognizes that the sum of his life is being taken and that should he die, with the exception of a few weeks or months of remembrance (if that), that sum, that life, will have no further value. He will not be called to explain himself at a Heavenly court of justice. It will all be over. It will all have come to this! I can think of no better depiction of these moments than in Sergio Leone's *Once Upon a Time in the West*. Near the end of the film, Charles Bronson's character Harmonica faces the vicious Frank played by Henry Fonda. Many years before, Frank had sadistically hung Harmonica's brother. After jamming a harmonica in his mouth, Frank forced Harmonica to balance his strung-up brother on his shoulders, until the brother kicked him out and was lynched. Harmonica, apparently, spent his life in a search for revenge. The scene in which the two finally face-off takes almost ten minutes of the film. Most of the camera shots are extreme close-ups of the eyes of the two men. In flashbacks we see Harmonica's recollection of the hanging of his brother. In Frank's eyes we see only the steely sizing up of a competitor, a check for the location of the sun, etc. After Frank is fatally shot in the gunfight and he lies dying on the ground, his only concern is for the identity of Harmonica. To which Harmonica responds by pulling the harmonica from a cord around his neck and jamming it into Frank's mouth. At the moment of death, Frank's eyes indicate that he remembers the killing of Harmonica's brother among so many he has committed and he almost seems to express an approval of the revenge taken out on him.

V

Although I am not a social anthropologist or sociologist, I want to venture a connection that may account in some respects for the Western's approach to and obsession with death. It is the impact of Mexican culture on the southwestern United States and on the writers and directors of Westerns. I lived for thirteen years in San Antonio, Texas, a city strongly influenced by the traditional Mexican folkways. One of the most important dates on the calendar is November 2, *Dia de los Muertos*, the Day of the Dead. Kearl describes this "death-rich cultural tradition" as reflecting "the fusion of Indian and Catholic legacies."[16] Mexicans even describe themselves as "seduced by death." But it is not morbidity that flows over their culture, it is death under the aspect of celebration. "On All Souls' Day . . . the deceased are honored and revered . . . By midafternoon families and friends gather to share prayers at family altars, drink wine, and reminisce about the lives of the deceased."[17] These picnic-like celebrations generally take place in the cemeteries and graveyards where the deceased are buried. A Hispanic writer for the San Antonio newspaper, Ricardo Sanchez, described *Dia de los Muertos* as "an existential affirmation of the lives and contributions made by all who have existed."[18] He went on to say that the celebrations are "the affirmation of life as the means of realizing its promise while preparing to someday die." The latter sentiment is carried throughout the Western.

Some of the filmmakers, Sam Peckinpah in particular, are Mexico-intoxicated. Peckinpah said, "Mexico has always meant something special to me . . . Everything important in my life has been linked to Mexico one way or another. The country has a special effect on me . . . In Mexico it's all out front—the color, the life, the warmth . . . It's direct. It's real. Whatever it is, they don't confuse it with anything else."[19] Little wonder Peckinpah would give us *The Wild Bunch* with its extreme consciousness of death. In its opening sequences we witness the mass slaughter of townspeople during a foiled robbery, while the children of the town are enjoying the killing of scorpions by thousands of ants. As the Bunch rides away, one of their gang is unable to continue, so the leader, Pike Bishop, shoots him. When there is talk of a burial, the idea is ridiculed by Dutch. Death rides with the Bunch throughout the film, not only because they are dealing in it, but because they, or at least Pike and Dutch, are profoundly aware of the fact that they are anachronisms, living on borrowed time. They talk of a last job and then retirement, but none of them believes it. They sense they will die brutally.

VI

Mary Midgley points out that the chief figure in a tragedy should display "every kind of quality except the one kind whose absence must ruin it."[20] She quotes from Milton's descriptions of Satan to show that even the epitome of evil "is torn with doubt and inner conflict," and that his grandeur "depends on the familiar good qualities . . . notably on virtues such as courage."[21] As will be discussed in the next chapter, Aristotle would not have called it courage (though perhaps he would have allowed bravery), nonetheless her point is well taken. The villains of the Westerns, at least those mentioned above, do, in fact, genuinely display the "familiar good qualities." But there is another point that Midgley makes about Satan's villainy in *Paradise Lost* that does not seem to fit the Rikers or the Mormon elders in *Riders of the Purple Sage* and their ilk in Westerns. Satan's primary evil motive is "ever to do ill out of sole delight, As being the contrary of his high will Whom we resist."[22] In other words, Satan's tragic flaw, which is Christian pride not Greek *hubris,* is evidenced in *Paradise Lost* as reactive meanness. His *modus operandi* is to learn what God wants and then do otherwise.

Satan's flaws, pride and envy, limit his actions in such a way that they are dependent on the acts and will of God. His central motives "are negative in two converging ways. They are destructive, and empty of positive content in the sense that they do not subserve any other, more constructive aims."[23] The villains of Westerns, generally, are not evil in that way. Although they are reacting to the influx of what they regard as undesirables in their midst, they do not, at least at first, allow the positive acts of the settlers or the independent miners or the small ranchers to determine their actions. Also, though they are cruel, they are not simply malignantly mean. They are more complex than that. They are replete with positive motives and long-term constructive aims. They simply cannot fit the intruders into their long-term plans. The valley isn't big enough. In *Shane,* for example, Riker visits the Starrett homestead and makes an offer to Starrett.

> Riker: You can run your cattle with mine. What's more, I'll buy your homestead. Set a price you think is reasonable. You'll find me reasonable. Is that fair?
> Starrett: You've made things pretty tough for us, Riker, and us in the right all the time.
> Riker: Right? You in the right? Look, Starrett. When I came to this country you weren't much older than your boy there. We had rough times, me and other men that are mostly dead now. I got a bad shoul-

der yet from a Cheyenne arrowhead. We made this country, found it, and we made it . . . Cattle we brought in were hazed off by Indians and rustlers. Don't bother you much anymore because we handled them. We made a safe range out of this. Some of us died doin' it, but we made it. And then people move in . . . fence off my range, fence me off from water. Some of them, like you, plow ditches, take out irrigation water, and so the creek runs dry sometimes. I got to move my stock because of it. And you say we have no right to the range. The men that did the work and ran the risk have no right? I take you for a fair man, Starrett.

VII

The westerner's struggles, unlike those of the Christian tragic hero, though they may spring from internal conflicts, are seldom settled internally. We struggle more with Ethan Edward's psyche than he ever does. We never see Shane pondering his fate or worrying about his internal conflicts. There is no "To be or not to be" soliloquy. He obviously has fallen in love with Marion, but much as Ethan must have recognized the impossibility of his love for Martha being fully requited, Shane keeps his distance and steps in where he clearly recognizes his duty. Will Kane in *High Noon* does undergo for us both the external and the internal struggles of a westerner against the wall. But he spends less time in deciding what he will do than in trying to insure a successful carrying out of it. Most of the film is taken up with Kane's unsuccessful attempts to assemble the townspeople of Hadleyville in their own defense and assisting him in doing what he, and he alone, has determined he must do: face Frank Miller and his gang.

Obsession with revenge is a standard Western plot, but revenge does not drive the hero to doom, it propels him to transcend ordinary humans (something that also happens for Ahab in *Moby Dick*). Ahab falls from grace because of his obsession with courting death by seeking revenge against the white whale he believes maimed him for reasons of personal malice. Auden notes that by doing so Ahab "has made his salvation a much harder task, for he is now required to forgive the whale personally."[24] His achievement of grace would have been far easier had he merely attributed the whale's devouring of his leg and tearing his body apart to the clumsiness of a huge dumb creature. That obsession with personal revenge eventually slams all the doors of grace in Ahab's scar-torn face. The westerner, on the other hand, typically ascends to a state of grace by his vengeful death-risking and death-dealing acts. The achievement of or ascension to a state of grace in such moments is, perhaps, the only viable explanation for the ability of the hero to survive the barrage of bullets.

Consider the final scenes of *Unforgiven*. The very title of the film reminds us that the characters, all of them, are unforgiven and will remain so. Indeed, they are unforgivable. They will not and cannot be forgiven. William Munny brags, "I've killed women, and children . . . killed just about everything that walks or crawls at one time or another." Now he has come to kill the sheriff. He isn't contrite. He has no remorse. Death is his way of life, the only occupation at which he has ever been any good. Then, in a remarkable scene that shares some similarities with one in *Pale Rider*, he slaughters, by my count, six men who are gathered in a saloon, a relatively small space, and he never receives a scratch. (Beauchamp, the writer of dime western novels, says that he killed five, but he seems not to be counting the owner of the saloon who was killed by Munny before the gunfight erupts.) By the point in *Pale Rider* where the slaughter in the cafe occurs there is little doubt that the Preacher personifies Death and will not be killed or even wounded. He is Death and thereby has the grace of death. William Munny, on the other hand, is an ordinary human being. What makes Munny invulnerable?

"Grace" has a number of different meanings, though they seem to basically relate to its Latin roots in *gratia*, favor. For the Christian, especially the Protestant Christian, grace is an undeserved salvation, an unearned gift from God. It is what is conveyed in the mercy of God, a pardon for the sinful. And insofar as it cannot be purchased by human deeds, it is *gratis*.

It would be totally out of character for such a conception of grace to play any significant role in a Western. And, indeed, it does not. Instead, the grace of William Munny, Shane, Link Jones, and a number of other westerners is self-conferred. They achieve it through their own actions. For example, I think it makes sense to say that William Munny's very ruthlessness and cold-bloodedness puts him in a state of grace when he enters the saloon at the end of the film. He knows, as he earlier tells the Schofield Kid, "It's a hell of a thing to kill a man. You take away everything he's got . . . and everything he's ever going to have." But he, unlike most other men, does not shrink from, give pause to, performing such "a hell of a thing." Like J. B. Books of *The Shootist*, he will not blink. Further, he responds to the Kid's "I guess he had it coming," with a cold and flat "We all have it coming, Kid." And to the sheriff's "I don't deserve to die like this . . . I was building a house," he spits out, "Deserves got nothing to do with it." At some level he grasps that death is the annihilation of everyone's life and that life is always "lived at the edge of death";[25] that understanding, coupled with his cold-blooded acceptance of what that means for him, raises him to a state of both dignity and grace. Until that point in the film, he is anything but a person of dignity and he certainly is not in a state of grace.

Munny's acceptance of the role of avenger of the unwarranted killing of his friend Ned is not without considerable feeling, but he overcomes those normal human feelings and hardens himself to the murders he commits. The contrast between what he is able to do and what the Kid cannot do is stark. The Kid also has murdered someone, though it took three shots while the victim was relieving himself in an outhouse. But the Kid cannot harden his heart, he wants sentimental explanations, he cannot sacrifice his emotions. He wants to know that the specific person he killed deserved to die, had it coming. But, of course, he didn't, or he didn't any more than does anyone else.[26] Munny understands what the Kid doesn't because Munny knows what it is to be unforgiven and to suffer without hope of salvation. He can move with a purposeful, easy elegance (another definition of "grace") that others cannot affect because their hearts and consequently their motivations are bound up in so many other commitments. They allow feelings to interrupt their concentration. They think about more than what the specific violent moment requires. The westerner confers on himself the grace that protects him. He has taught himself to set aside, at least for the crucial moments, his normal human feelings. He hardens his heart, and in doing so, elevates himself above that ordinary run of men who blink.

Tompkins refers to this hardening of the heart process in the westerner as "the need for numbness." She writes, "The death of the heart, or rather, it's [*sic*] scarification and eventual sacrifice, is what the Western genre, more than anything else, is about. The numbing of the capacity to feel, which allows the hero to inflict pain on others, requires the sacrifice of his own heart, a sacrifice kept hidden under his toughness, which is inseparable from his heroic character."[27] In large measure, she is correct. The process of steeling oneself to do what one normally would not, even could not, do is required for self-conferred grace. The villain, when he is also a westerner, such as Wilson, has also hardened his heart, numbed his feelings, but he has done so to the point where there are no feelings left. Wilson smiles both when he kills the hapless homesteader Torrey in a gunfight he has provoked and when he faces Shane in the final showdown. There is no sign of pain in his face, hardly any show of emotion at all. He is the epitome of the cold-blooded killer. He has no heart. Frank, in *Once Upon a Time in the West,* tries to show us a similar numbness, though, admittedly, it is harder to accept it in Henry Fonda because of the natural warmth of feeling in his blue eyes. Sergio Leone's directoral technique of moving in to extreme close-ups of Fonda's eyes at the final gunfight has the drawback of focusing on the eyes of an actor who most certainly had not lost his heart to terminal numbness. The rest of Fonda's movements, particularly his facial movements, however, do not betray the intended depiction of dead-hearted villainy. Charles Bronson, on the other hand, in the same film, shows us exactly what the hero must do to himself to successfully carry off the killing of another person, even one who deserves to die. We are allowed to see his mental focus on the event that led him to seek out Frank: the gruesome hanging of his brother, and the single-mindedness that drained the emotion and the feeling from him, so that he could successfully perform the violent deed. In *Man of the West*, as Tompkins notes,[28] Gary Cooper, as Link Jones, does an especially good job of showing us how a man undergoes the self-inflicted hardening of his heart. "The human body is the best picture of the human soul," Wittgenstein said.[29] And the human face is the body's best portrait of what has and is going on emotionally inside the person. Cooper's face in most of his Westerns draws us a picture of torture and extreme pain. We see how much it must hurt him to do what he does, to beat and kill other humans. Still, we see his resolve to do it, not to be deterred by ordinary human emotions, to be tough where others likely would soften.

The westerner hero, unlike his counterpart villain, still displays feelings and emotions. He is not emotionally bankrupt, but he has put his emotions aside. He has overcome them in rising to the moment of killing. Shane, the Preacher, Harmonica, and William Munny face the shoot-out with an almost superhuman confidence that is a product of their intentional damming of the rush of emotions that others must feel in those moments. They bestow grace upon themselves by transcending themselves, by becoming something both less and more than human.

But there must eventually be a cost, a high psychological price, to be paid for such grace. What it is, of course, is yet another death in Westerns: the death of ordinary human feelings. The hero's noble behavior is a kind of sacrifice: the sacrifice of his emotional side and therefore a significant part of his humanity. In *Unforgiven* William Munny, after having been brutally beaten near to death and nursed back to health by the prostitutes who began the whole vengeance cycle, has the following conversation with the prostitute who was disfigured:

Prostitute: Would you like a free one?
Munny: No, I guess not.
Prostitute: I didn't mean me . . .
Munny: You ain't ugly like me. It's just that we both got scars. But you're a beautiful woman and if I was to want a free one, I'd want it

with you, I guess, more than with them other two. It's that I can't on
account of my wife.
Prostitute: Your wife?
Munny: You see . . .
Prostitute: Is she back in Kansas?
Munny: Yeah, she's watching over my young ones.

Munny's wife is dead, but he has not yet so hardened his heart, blocked his
emotions, that he cannot find an appropriate response. After the killing of
Ned, he will have hardened himself, bolstered with whiskey, to enter Greeley's saloon and shoot down six men coldheartedly.

VIII

Perhaps the tragedy of the westerner hero is the tragedy of necessarily dirty
moral hands. If that is the case, he might not be too different from Machiavelli's prince. Michael Walzer has defined the "dirty hands" problem as one
in which a person in a position of authority is "forced to choose between
upholding an important moral principle and avoiding some looming disaster."[30] If the person upholds the moral principle(s), the disaster will befall
and he or she will have failed in his or her political duty, the duty of the
office he or she holds. If he or she acts expediently to ward off the looming
disaster by violating the moral principle(s), he or she has acted immorally,
hence dirty hands. Machiavelli's prince, famously, had to learn not to be
good and, it should not be forgotten, to accept the moral consequences of
his wickedness. The prince, he tells us, "ought not to mind the disgrace of
being called cruel."[31] Sometimes the law is inadequate to achieve the
prince's desired outcome and the prince must imitate the actions of the
tiger, the beast, and do by force what he could not do by law. There is
another element in this Machiavellian picture that also helps us understand
the "tragedy" of the westerner. It is not enough that the hero (or the
prince) be willing to forgo moral constraint and morally dirty his hands in
a good cause. "He must be prepared to do wrong if necessary."[32]

Montaigne carries the antiabsolutist moral position in the dirty hands
defense further, "[A] man must do wrong in detail if he wishes to do right
on the whole and commit injustices in small matters if he hopes to deal out
justice in great . . . [N]ature herself in most of her works goes against justice
. . . [T]heft, sacrilege, and all sorts of crimes are lawful for the sage if he
knows that they are profitable to him."[33] Setting aside the comments on
the sage, we can apply Montaigne's description to the predicament of the

westerner hero who is called upon by both circumstances and his skills. He is uniquely qualified to do wrong in detail to do right on the whole. What often makes matters worse for the hero is that typically, deep in his hardened heart, he does not want to see the outcome that is "the morally right one" occur. That is one of the more important reasons why he must harden his heart, to dispel his emotions and "do wrong in detail."

In *The Man Who Shot Liberty Valance* we have a perfect example of the dirty hands hero violating not only generally accepted moral codes, but his own code of behavior, to bring about an outcome that he, probably begrudgingly, acknowledges is "right on the whole." Tom Doniphon, played by John Wayne, is the epitome of the westerner. Though he saved the easterner Ransom Stoddard's life early in the film by bringing Ranse's battered body to town to be nursed by Tom's girlfriend Hallie, he despises virtually everything for which the dude stands. Actually Stoddard does not physically stand very often in the early parts of the film's lengthy flashback sequence. He is almost always prone, and Doniphon looms over him, as does the villain, Liberty Valance. Doniphon finds himself regularly bolstering Stoddard and protecting him from attack by Valance. He does this even though he comes to believe that Hallie is in love with Stoddard, a belief that probably is unfounded, though she is sympathetic to him and certainly admires his education and mothers him back to strength. In any event, when Valance finally meets Stoddard on the dark streets of Shinbone for a showdown, it is Doniphon who kills Valance by shooting him with a rifle from the shadows of an alley, an act of murder. Stoddard is credited with killing Valance and is launched on a successful political career, one for which he seems aptly suited. When Doniphon later tells Stoddard that Doniphon had killed Valance, he responds to the question: "How could you do it?" with "Because I could live with it." Which, of course, is just what the Machiavellian prince should say. The prince, as Walzer reminds us,[34] can, however, expect to pay an eternal price for his immorality. The westerner has no immortal soul to be punished, no afterlife, no next-worldly Hell. And so, Doniphon's princely proclamation turns out to be a lie. Doniphon cannot live with it. His "wrong in detail" makes Shinbone and the territory safe for law and order and statehood, but not for him. His killing of Liberty Valance amounts to his destroying his own liberty. He destroys himself and what he most cares about. First he burns down the cabin he has been building for himself and Hallie and then he drifts into becoming a drunken bum who has lost his personal dignity and his moral authority in Shinbone. Still, his act was heroic in the best sense of the term. He sacrificed everything that he cared about to do something he most clearly believed was wrong: shoot Liberty Valance from the shadows. And he did it for a morally good cause, even though he does not care about the cause. In fact, if he has any other motivation for saving Stoddard, it is that he believes that Hallie wants him to do it. He is, in large measure, a suffering, sacrificing, servant to the relentless march of easterner progress.

The dirty hands of the westerner hero are, at least partially, cleansed by his sacrifice, not through an eternity in Hell. He sacrifices long-lasting relationships with other humans, and he sacrifices the things he most cares about, e.g., the wilderness. He travels on West, or, as in the case of Tom Doniphon who has run out of territory, he self-destructs. He has taken on what Walzer and Weber call "the diabolic forces lurking in all violence."[35] He has internalized them, but his hardened heart and practiced extreme loneliness is something of a match for them. He absorbs those forces, constrains them, though the struggle is often evident in his face, and then he unleashes them at propitious moments. He must pay the price of solitude. Yet, he seems prepared to do so and even willingly accepts his condition.

I think Tompkins is just wrong when she implies that the westerner hero cannot like living with himself.[36] He is not resigned to being a suffering servant. He never thinks, "if it weren't for the solitude of my existence and my appreciation of silence, I'd have a lot better time in life." In this respect at least, and usually if not at all times, he knows himself, which is to know his limits as well as his powers. His limits are those set by what he cares most about, which in simple terms is the wilderness and all that means. What it means, in part, is freedom, freedom to continue to ride West until you buck off. To have that sort of freedom one must pay certain costs, and those include exactly the sort of social amenities in which Tompkins places such stock: going home to dinner, looking at pictures, sewing, keeping house, and playing the fool. No woman ever has to worry about what it would be like to live with "this edgy, introverted person, with hair-trigger reflexes and an undigestible past."[37] Shane won't come back. Sarah has her night with the Preacher so she won't have to live her life wondering what sex with him would have been like, though the Preacher seems to have had no similar concerns about her. Tom Doniphon would never have married Hallie even had he not burned down the room he was building for her. Ethan Edwards will never settle into a family and a home life. And so it goes. Tragic? Perhaps. Heroic? Yes. Noble? I think so. Or at least some of the westerner heroes display the characteristics and "virtues" Nietzsche ascribes to what he calls the noble.

IX

In *Beyond Good and Evil*, Nietzsche tells us that the human race has only advanced because of the work of aristocratic societies. His aristocrats (the noble) are the ancestors of barbarians: "men of prey who were still in possession of unbroken strength of will and lust for power . . . [They] hurled themselves upon the weaker, more civilized, more peaceful races, perhaps traders or cattle raisers . . . In the beginning the noble caste was always the barbarian caste: . . . they were more whole human beings (which also means, at every level, 'more whole beasts')."[38] Life, says Nietzsche, is essentially appropriation, injury, overpowering of what is weaker, suppression, hardness, imposition of one's own forms, exploitation. Exploitation belongs to the essence of what lives. It is "a basic organic function; it is a consequence of the will to power, which is after all the will of life."[39]

Nietzsche thinks, or wants us to think, that he is describing an ancient heroic society like that of the *Iliad*. He is certainly not, as MacIntyre has noted.[40] The Homeric hero is dominated by his role in the system of roles that fully constitutes his society. He is socially created. Nietzsche's ideal noble is a self-creator. Nietzsche is what the ancient was definitely not, an individualist, albeit, an individualist who is fiercely critical of the sort of individualism that emerged out of the works of philosophers like Locke and that has dominated our liberal democratic institutional thinking from the seventeenth century to the present.

As is well known, Nietzsche goes on in part 9 of *Beyond Good and Evil* to distinguish between the master and slave types of moralities. It is only to master morality, as he explicates it, that we need look to see the dominant traits of certain westerner heroes enumerated. They are especially evident in many of the characters played by Clint Eastwood, nowhere more obviously than in *High Plains Drifter*. There is also something of the Nietzschean noble in John Russell, Paul Newman's character in *Hombre*.

The noble person, Nietzsche insists, despises those that are not noble. He sets himself off, separates himself, from those that are not proud. He has contempt for the cowardly, the petty, the anxious. The bulk of *Hombre*, the stagecoach ride and long walk across the desert, is spent in displaying the weaknesses in the characters of the passengers. They are cowardly, petty, scared, avaricious. The contrast to Russell, who keeps himself apart from the rest and who has nothing but contempt for them, is crystal clear.

Nietzsche detests those who humble themselves, begging flatterers, "the doglike people who allow themselves to be maltreated," and "above all the liars."[41] Nietzsche tells us that the nobility of ancient Greece referred to themselves as "We truthful ones." Recall Will Anderson in *The Cowboys*, expressing such sentiments to Amos Watts. "I hate a liar."

The Nietzschean noble "honors himself as one who is powerful, also as one who has power over himself, who knows how to speak and be silent, who delights in being severe and hard with himself and respects all severity and hardness." The description fits the Eastwood characters in *The Good, The Bad, and The Ugly*, and *High Plains Drifter*.

Nietzsche quotes approvingly from a Scandinavian saga in which the hero tells us that Wotan had put a hard heart in his chest. The noble, as with the westerner hero, has learned to harden his heart. He is proud that "he is *not* made for pity."[42] One of the lessons Shane teaches Little Joey, Books teaches Gillam, Will Penny teaches Horace is that he is not to be pitied for living the life he leads. As Conn Vallian tells Susannah about his lonesome life in the wilderness, "To me, it's the best, always the best."

A Nietzschean noble person eschews pity of any kind. Though Christian morality might urge one to act for the sake of others out of pity for their condition or that one should help others disinterestedly, that is, without regard to who they are, such motives are utterly rejected by the Nietzschean noble. He helps the unfortunate, not from pity for their downtrodden condition, but because he is prompted by an overflow, an excess of his own power to do so. He does not go to their aid because he cares how they will otherwise fare. He virtually cannot help himself from helping them because in doing so his own power is actualized for and in himself. They are occasions for his expression of his own virtue. This seems especially clear in *Hombre*. Russell insults his fellow stagecoach passengers throughout the film and proves to them, especially the males, that they are utter cowards.

> Russell: It's your wife down there, you gonna cut her loose? Mendez, you gonna save her? Billy Lee, what's your last name? You gonna go down there? This one (*indicating Dr. Favor*) won't, that's his woman, but he won't do it. He doesn't care enough about his own woman, but maybe someone else does, huh? All right, you lady, you worry more about his wife than he does. Go down there, cut her loose, start back up. Get shot in the back or the front if the Mexican by the trough does it. In the back or in the front, but one way or the other . . .

He, however, takes up the task of trying to save Mrs. Favor. It costs him his life. Why does he do it? He cannot help doing it. It is not his choice. At least it is not his choice in the first instance. The only passenger willing to try to make the trade of the stolen money for Mrs. Favor is the less than respectable woman played by Diane Cilento. Russell, however, has no intention of allowing the outlaws to get their hands on the money. He will rescue Mrs. Favor by trading a sack of old cloth for her. The money is to be returned to the Apache reservation from which it was stolen by Dr. Favor. Russell descends down the mountainside to free Mrs. Favor fully aware he is more than likely to be killed. It is not that he has been shamed into the action. If Nietzsche is right, he experiences himself "to be that which first accords honor to things." He is "value creating." His act is a form of "self-glorification." We see in his face, and that of the Eastwood characters mentioned above, both the hardened heart and "the feeling of fullness, of power that seeks to overflow."[43]

Nietzsche's noble also evidences a fundamental hostility against selflessness. *High Plains Drifter* provides us with such a character. The stranger who enters Lago and will save it from the tyranny of a vicious gang bent on revenge against the town, does not do so out of altruistic motives. Far from it. He has scorn for altruism and he has scorn for virtually all of the people of Lago. In the first few minutes of the film he rides into town, kills three men, and rapes a woman. Then he demands total obedience from the citizens to his every whim, and he further insults them by making a dwarf the sheriff. In terror and the hope he will protect them, they accede to his every demand, even when he makes them feel utterly ridiculous. He quashes a minor revolt and then orders them to paint the entire town a bright red. Nonetheless, he does kill the outlaws and saves the town, though not all of its citizens. He is a kind of avenging angel, perhaps even a reincarnation of the town's former lawman who the townspeople failed to support when the same gang rampaged in Lago years before. In any event, his mission is more personal than social. The town's rescue is only incidental to his own purposes. He is bent on punishing and humiliating the people of Lago as much as avenging himself on the gang. But he does save the town.

Nietzsche's noble is a man of honor, and he has the capacity for and the duty of long gratitude and long revenge. He also has a certain necessity for having enemies, says Nietzsche, as drainage for his own envy, quarrelsomeness, and exuberance.

As already noted, Nietzsche's conception of the aristocratic noble and his values is a nineteenth century creation steeped in individualism and not a product of careful research into the ancient Greek society, as Nietzsche would like us to believe. That aside, the impact of such a conception on the Western genre that has roots in the same time period as Nietzsche's writings, a period of philosophical and literary reaction to the Christian domestic ideal, is to be expected. I think there is something of the Nietzschean noble in every one of the westerner heroes. But only in a few cases are we confronted with the full-blown model, and those film heroes seem more monomaniacal and less convincing as heroes than those with less hardened hearts. We used to call them antiheroes. They enter the film already emotionally frozen, and they seldom thaw out. For example, *A*

Fistful of Dollars is crammed with scenes in which Clint Eastwood's character displays a near moribund heart, though he does reveal one soft spot in dealing with a child and his mother. He responds to "I'd like you to feel at home," with "I've never found home that great." He treats his killing four men as a matter of course, perfunctorily telling the coffin-maker to make enough coffins. Then he takes fatal revenge for the way members of one of the town's two rival gangs harassed him and frightened his mule when he first entered the town.

X

The westerner heroes, whether or not Nietzschean nobles, do evidence a character trait that flies in the face of the traditional Christian virtues. They are prideful individuals. They care deeply about their dignity and self-respect. Kant argued that "our duties towards ourselves are of primary importance . . . ; for . . . it is obvious that nothing can be expected from a man who dishonors his own person. He who transgresses against himself loses his manliness and becomes incapable of doing his duty towards his fellows . . . he who has transgressed his duty towards himself, can have no inner worth whatever."[44] For Kant, "self-respect in comparison with others constitutes noble pride. A low opinion of oneself in relation to others is not humility; it is a sign of a little spirit and of a servile character."[45] But Kant's "noble pride" falls far short of the sort of pride that is a typical trait in the character of the westerner hero.

   Richard Taylor defines pride as "the justified love of oneself."[46] The justification is crucial. Put another way, "genuinely proud people perceive themselves as better than others, and their pride is justified because their perception is correct."[47] Kant, of course, will have none of this. He writes, "We all have the right to demand of a man that he should not think himself superior."[48] In *Pride and Prejudice*, Jane Austen, through the mouth of Elizabeth, describes Darcy as "Indeed he has no improper pride."[49] His pride is appropriate to him. In what ways are proud people better than others? Richard Taylor, I think correctly, maintains that pride, understood as a self-admiring grasp of one's personal excellence, is "the summation of most of the other virtues, since it presupposes them."[50] What the justifiably proud person evidences is the realization of the virtues, particularly, I suppose, those that Aristotle identified in the *Nicomachean Ethics*: temperance, courage, justice, liberality, magnificence, and what Aristotle calls "greatness of soul." Aristotle's "great-souled man," in fact, is a close relative to the proud person as described by Richard Taylor, the family resemblance shows in the shared trait of possessing a sort of summation of most of the other virtues.

There are echoes, not always so faint, of Nietzsche's noble in the standard descriptions of the Aristotelian great-souled man. MacIntyre describes him as follows: "He despises honors offered by common people. He is gracious to inferiors. He repays benefits so as not to be put under obligations . . . He speaks his mind without fear or favor, because he has a poor opinion of others and would not care to conceal his opinion."[51]

Genuinely proud people, as Richard Taylor notes, are not vain or conceited. Jane Austen reminds us, "Vanity is a weakness indeed. But pride—where there is a real superiority of mind, pride will be always under good regulation."[52] Nor are proud people arrogant. Arrogance is a trait exhibited toward other people. Pride is an inner-directed feeling of approbation, of self-satisfaction. An arrogant person is outer-directed. For example, typically arrogant people entertain themselves by belittling others in order to draw attention to their own accomplishments. Gabriele Taylor is wrong on two counts when she tells us that "the type of pride exemplified by Mr. Darcy is arrogance, or pride the sin."[53] In the first place, Mr. Darcy is most definitely not outer-directed. He is predominately an inner-directed person. He does not belittle others to draw attention to himself. He views himself as superior to others, particularly the bumpkins at the ball at Netherfield, and in that he is surely correct. He stands apart from them not to call attention to himself, but because he cannot see himself mingling with them. In the second place, Gabriele Taylor is wrong to assimilate arrogance to pride and identify it as the Christian sin. Pride itself is the Christian sin for it is not, in Kant's terms, "grounded in the worth of humanity." It is not derived from comparison with the moral law. Indeed, the person of pride does not consult the moral law as a gauge of his or her worth.

The standard villains of Westerns generally are arrogant, though the Clint Eastwood character in *High Plains Drifter* certainly evidences no small degree of it. On the other hand, John Russell in *Hombre* is not arrogant. The more convincing, and, I think, menacing villains, such as those played by Richard Boone in *The Tall T* and in *Hombre*, are also men of pride and display little arrogance. Shane and Will Kane are men of pride lacking in arrogance and also lacking in those other traits that are sometimes confused with pride: egotism and conceit.

Pride, Richard Taylor tells us, is tested in responses to extreme danger or in instances involving "humiliation at the hands of enemies."[54] These are borne by the proud person with fortitude and without self-pity. Consider humiliation at the hands of enemies. In *The Magnificent Seven*, the mercenary American gunfighters return to the small Mexican village they have been paid to protect from a band of bandits only to discover that the bandits have captured the town. They are stripped of their guns and led out of town in disgrace. Their capturers release them and return their guns on a hilltop road above the village. As they strap on their guns, they discuss whether they will ride on or return to the village to do the job they were paid to do. The tenor of their discussion is a primer on how the proud person reacts to humiliation at the hands of an enemy. They know that even their own life is not worth living if they must sacrifice honor and pride to live it. Six of the seven strap on their guns and prepare to try to take back the village from the bandits. The seventh rides off, but he rides back in the heat of the ensuing battle, guns blazing, and gives his life in the cause.

In *Lonesome Dove* we have a memorable example of another test of the proud person. Richard Taylor tells us that a proud person "would never want [his life] prolonged beyond the point where the virtues upon which pride rests have become debilitated," for a person of pride would prefer to die "ten years too soon than ten days too late."[55] Gus has been attacked by Indians and is severely wounded by arrows in both legs. He is taken to a doctor in a Montana town. The doctor amputates one of Gus's legs. Gus awakes to discover the amputation. The doctor tells him that the other one must also be cut off.

> Doctor: You'll die if we don't take it off.
> Gus: You ain't gettin' my other leg, sawbones.
> Doctor: I assure you sir, the alternative is gloomy. You seem to have a feelin' for music. Why don't you give yourself a few more years of listenin' to whores playin' the piano?
> Gus: Why don't you just shut up and go get some whiskey?
> Doctor: I should operate today. I could have that leg off in fifteen minutes.
> Gus: No sir. . . .
> (*His old and good friend Woodrow Call arrives.*)
> Gus: Took you long enough to get here, Woodrow.
> Doctor: I told him it should come off.
> Woodrow: We can still take it off.
> Gus (*pulls gun*): No sir.
> Woodrow: You wouldn't kill me for tryin' to save your life.
> Gus: No, but I'll durn sure disable you.
> Woodrow: I never figured you for a suicide, Gus. What are your old legs for anyway? You don't like to do nothin' but sit on the porch and drink whiskey.
> Gus: I like to kick a pig every once and a while. How'd I do that?

Doctor: It's much too late now. I wouldn't bother him about it anymore.

Gus: Pour us a drink, Woodrow. Arguing with you always makes me thristy.

Doctor: I'll leave now.

Gus: Why don't you relax? You can't save me. You ain't goin' to become a drunkard over me, are you?

Woodrow: No, go ahead and die, if you want to.

Gus: So, you act like you hold it against me. I walked this earth my whole life with my pride, you see. Now if that's lost, then let the rest be lost with it . . .

But these tests of pride are, by and large, focused on responses to adversity. One of the positive tests of the virtue of pride, as noted by Richard Taylor, is that the proud person is not taken in by the untested claims of religions and ideologies. In the Westerns, the hero is slow to accept any ideological position and, as noted earlier, has suspicion, even contempt, for religious faiths and those who preach them.

The same disdain for religious doctrines extends in the proud westerner to moral principles as well, which is not to say that the westerner is antimoral. Not in the least. Instead, and rather like the Nietzschean noble and the Aristotelian great-souled man, the westerner hero does what he does not because he is a rule-follower, nor even, for that matter, a code-follower or consulter, but because he firmly believes that it is the worthy thing to be done in the circumstances. Being the worthy thing in the circumstances is being the thing that is worthy of that person in the circumstances. Morality for the westerner hero is a matter of personal judgment and its governing factor is shame.

XI

The hero will not allow himself to be shameful. To act shamefully is to dishonor oneself, to reduce one's personal worth, in fact, to have, in Kant's terms, "no inner worth whatever." Shame and honor dominate the ethics of the westerner while they do not play much of a role at all in the lives of the other characters in the films (and most of us). Shame-avoidance and honor are sufficient reasons for action. Rules, laws, and codes are superfluous to persons of genuine pride and self-respect, such as J. B. Books, although they may be able to provide an eager pupil with a rough and ready encapsulation of how they act toward others.

At the end of *Ride the High Country*, Gil Westrum escapes from his old partner, Steve Judd, who is taking him to a sheriff because Judd caught Westrum trying to steal the gold shipment they were guarding. Judd, however, is shot in a gun battle with a gang, and Westrum rides back to try to save him. After the fight is over and Judd lies dying, Westrum agrees to take the gold to its rightful owners. He does so not because he now has come to see the virtue in the Mosaic prohibition against stealing, but because he recognizes in the sacrifice of his old friend where his own honor lies and what he must do to preserve or restore it. He will do it because not to do it would be shameful. He would, in Kant's terms, be dishonoring his own person. The two old gunslingers have the following final conversation:

> Judd: How'd we figure? A thousand dollars a shot? Those boys surely made me a lot of money. They put 'em all in one spot. I don't want them to see this. I'll go it alone.
> Westrum: Don't worry about anything. I'll take care of it just like you would have.
> Judd: Hell, I know that. I always did. You just forgot it for awhile. So long partner.
> Westrum: I'll see ya later.

I have written at length elsewhere about the power of shame[56] and its virtues. I do not want to reiterate that here. However, it is important to note that there are two sides to shame, one of which I underemphasized in my other discussions of the topic. The etymology of "shame" reveals that it has to do with covering, veiling, or hiding oneself. Shame is provoked by the feeling or the belief or the knowledge that one has failed to achieve an expected goal, fallen short, been inferior or exposed a weakness one ought not have. The usual human response to such feelings, beliefs, or knowledge is to try to hide one's failure or hide oneself from others. Shame relates to seeing, seeing oneself and/or being seen by others. Insofar as how one thinks one is being seen by others is generally thought to be crucial to shame, we should expect that shame is dependent on a community for its ethical force. Shame seems to require an audience. Gabriele Taylor writes, "The audience . . . is primarily needed for an explanation of shame: in feeling shame the actor thinks of himself as having become an object of detached observation, and at the core to feel shame is to feel distress at being seen at all. *How* he is seen, whether he thinks of the audience as critical, approving, indifferent, cynical or naive is a distinguishable step and accounts for the different cases of shame."[57]

Though community- or audience-focused shame may be shame's

most common variety, and it certainly is evident in countries like Japan and in small town life in many European and American settings, there is a noncommunity-focused type of shame as well. It is personal-focused shame. The person who is personal-focused shameable, without reference to the views of others, may see his or her own acts as unworthy of himself or herself, as something for which he or she should be ashamed. Such shame is a matter of personal honor, self-worth. To see oneself as having fallen below one's own standards can, in truly proud persons, produce great shame. Others may be shamed as long as there is an audience. But, in the absence of an audience of other people, if the matter were purely private, they suffer no sense of shame for their failures. Personal-focused shame, however, can be a powerful controlling factor with respect to the behavior of a proud person who could not care one iota about public opinion.

Experiences of shame of both types are typically described as involving a devastating sensation of the loss or the slipping away of the identity one has tried to maintain and/or project to others. To be shamed is to be stripped of one's self-image. Helen Merrell Lynd writes about shame: "Like honor, shame is a multifaceted word. It includes the subjective feeling of the person and the objective nature of the act. Shame is defined as a wound to one's self-esteem, a painful feeling or sense of degradation excited by the consciousness of having done something unworthy of one's previous idea of one's own excellence . . . Shame is an experience that affects and is affected by the whole self. This whole-self involvement is one of its distinguishing characteristics and the one that makes it a clue to identity . . . [E]xperiences of shame throw a flooding light on what and who we are and what the world we live in is."[58] Suffering shame is an identity crisis and shame anxiety is the fear of radical isolation; in the case of the personal-focused variety, it is the fear of self-alienation, being an outcast, not of Poker Flat, but of oneself.

The proud person seeks to avoid self-focused shame. In an important sense, he or she is his or her own and only important audience. The quiet confidence of the westerner hero bespeaks such pride. The story lines make it evident. Westerner heroes ride in the shadow of self-alienation as much as they ride in the shadow of death. In *High Noon*, Will Kane could leave Hadleyville, indeed he starts to do so, and not stay to face the challenge of the Miller gang. Everyone urges him to leave. No one asks him to stay. His return has been described as an act of Kantian duty, which is, I think, an insufficient motivation for him and not strictly true to the story. When asked by his wife why he is returning, he offers weak prudential reasons, such as that wherever they go Miller will locate them. He might as well get it over with now rather than face Miller later. He certainly has no station or role duties in the matter. He has met his obligations as town marshal. He has already served out his term and his successor is to arrive the next day. He seems not to have consulted anything like the Categorical Imperative to determine if he could will what he is doing as a universal law.

Though Will Kane undeniably has a strong sense of duty, it is his pride that brings him back to town and to the final showdown with Frank Miller. The famous song from the film tells us that he must "be brave and . . . face a man that hates me or lie a coward, a craven coward in my grave." His concern is not whether everyone would have such a duty (though the song mentions being torn between love and duty). What he will do is heroic and so not within the scope of duty. The main motivator is the business about lying a coward in his grave, knowing himself for the rest of his life to have been a coward and being remembered as such. Obviously, if he does not face Miller on this Sunday, he will not then be killed by the Miller gang, so the concern about lying a coward in the grave reflects his understanding that evading the confrontation will diminish his own self-respect regardless of how long he might live. To himself, and perhaps himself alone, he will not have been sufficiently brave. He will have been, not just a coward, but a craven coward, and that is something too shameful for him to endure. He is his own audience, and it is personal-focused shame-avoidance that brings him out on the street to meet Frank Miller.

Kane is a man of pride, not the Christian sin, but the virtue that is a summation of most of the other virtues. So is Shane, Will Penny, Conn Vallian, Hondo, John Russell, and the majority of the other westerner heroes. They are motivated, not by what others might or might not think of them, but by what they will think of themselves. Where the Christian tragic hero typically is doomed by pride, a pride that often slips into arrogance, the westerner achieves success because of his pride, a justifiable confidence in himself. It elevates him to a state of grace.

Will Kane has doubts about whether he alone can defeat the Miller gang, and he even makes out his will before entering the fray (an extremely rare moment for a westerner hero!). Nevertheless he has confidence in himself, even though he may not be especially proud *of* his skills, for example, in gunfighting. In fact, in the standard Western plot the character who shows himself to be proud *of* his skills as a gunfighter is typically either killed off early or is reduced to running away from a showdown when confronted with a genuinely proud gunfighter.

There is a great difference between being a proud person and being proud *of* something one has or one has done. Again, Jane Austen in *Pride and Prejudice* displays the difference in the thoughts of Elizabeth, "For herself she was humbled; but she was proud of him. Proud that in a cause of compassion and honor, he had been able to get the better of himself."[59] Proud persons are not especially proud *of* their possessions, their accomplishments, or their skills. They seldom, if ever talk about them. And if they are pressed, as westerner heroes often are by children, they provide only extraordinarily sketchy accounts of their exploits. They do not revel in them. People who reveal themselves to be proud *of* their possessions, their accomplishments, their situations typically, in Westerns, are either villains or headed for a fall, probably a deadly one. Perhaps the Western's nod to the Christian tragic flaw is interpreting it as being proud *of* one's achievements, etc., rather than being proud, a person of pride.

The proud person accepts his status as something he deserves because of who he is. But he is quite unlike the person who is proud *of* the status he has achieved. Shane, for example, is a proud man. The Rikers are proud *of* what they have achieved in the valley. Shane tells Marion and Joe Starrett that only he is a match for both the Rikers and Wilson. He informs them as a mere matter of fact. It is not a boast. Shane is not especially proud *of* his skills. He and other westerner heroes take their particular talents for granted as something that they have, even as something that defines who they are. In fact, were they proud *of* them, they would not take them as a matter of course. Gabriele Taylor notes, "What a person is proud of in some way exceeds what in his own view he can expect as a matter of course."[60] Shane's skills as a gunfighter are up to, but do not surpass what he expects of himself. Similar things could be said of J. B. Books. Recall Gillom's shooting lesson in which the famous shootist admits to not being particularly fast or accurate. One cannot really be proud *of* doing what one expects of oneself.

To be proud *of* doing something a person must go, in Gabriele Taylor's terms, "beyond the person's norm of expectations."[61] The westerner hero's norm of expectations where his gunfighting and similar skills are concerned are high in the first place and they are met, but not exceeded. If one were to meet up with Shane in the mountains after the shootout in Graftons and asked him if he was proud of having killed Jack Wilson, he would probably respond just as he did to Little Joey. "That was Wilson, all right. He was fast, fast on the draw . . . I got to be goin' on . . . Man has to be what he is." In the Olympic Games in the 1990s this must have been something of a problem for the American men's basketball team, the "Dream Team." Even winning by extremely wide margins against the teams from the rest of the countries never could surpass the norm of expectations the team had for itself. Consequently, winning the Gold Medal was not as much to be proud *of* as they might have liked.

The westerner hero is neither a Greek nor a Christian tragic figure.

He is not a tragic figure at all. His story is not a tragic one, even if he proudly dies brutally, as Will Anderson does in *The Cowboys*. The real tragedy in Westerns is the great other death that they narrate: the death of death. I will take up that topic in chapter 6.

Notes

1. Tompkins, *West of Everything*, 26–27.
2. Aristotle, *Poetics*, trans. P. Wheelwright, in *Wheelwright's Aristotle* (New York, 1935).
3. W. H. Auden, "The Christian Tragic Hero," in *Exploring Philosophy*, ed. Peter French (Cambridge, Mass., 1970), 523–27.
4. Ibid., 523.
5. Aristotle, *Poetics*, 306.
6. Auden, "The Christian Tragic Hero," 524.
7. Ibid.
8. John Locke, *Second Treatise of Government* (1714), sec. 27. Locke wrote, "Whatsoever then he removes out of the state that Nature hath provided, and left it in, he hath mixed his labour with, and joyned to it something that is his own, and thereby makes it his Property. It being by him removed from the common state Nature placed it in, hath by this labour something annexed to it, that excludes the common right of other Men. For this no Man but he can have a right to what that is once joyned to, at least where there is enough and as good left in common for others."
9. Robert Nozick, *Anarchy, State, and Utopia.* (New York, 1974), 178.
10. Homer, *The Iliad*, trans. E. V. Rieu (New York, 1950), 405–6.
11. MacIntyre, *After Virtue*, 137.
12. Homer, *The Iliad*, 437.
13. Auden, "The Christian Tragic Hero," 523.
14. Ibid., 525.
15. Tompkins, *West of Everything*, 25.
16. Kearl, *Endings*, 39.
17. Ibid., 40.
18. Ricardo Sanchez, "Day of the Dead is also about Life," *San Antonio Express-News*, 1 November 1985, 1 E.
19. "Interview with Sam Peckinpah," *Playboy*, August 1972.
20. Mary Midgley, *Wickedness* (London, 1984), 133.
21. Ibid., 137.
22. John Milton, *Paradise Lost* (1667), bk. 1.
23. Midgley, *Wickedness*, 151.
24. Auden, "The Christian Tragic Hero," 525.
25. Tompkins, *West of Everything*, 25.
26. The act of the deceased that had provoked the bounty for his death was not

one that warranted his death as compensation, as the sheriff persuasively maintained from the beginning of the film.

27. Tompkins, *West of Everything*, 219.

28. Ibid., 218.

29. Ludwig Wittgenstein, *Philosophical Investigations* (London, 1953), 178.

30. Michael Walzer, "Political Action: The Problem of Dirty Hands," *Philosophy and Public Affairs* (1973–74): 160–80.

31. Nicolo Machiavelli, *The Prince*, trans. D. Wootton (Indianapolis, Ind., 1995), 51.

32. Ibid., 55.

33. Montaigne, *Essays*, 351.

34. Walzer, "Political Action: The Problem of Dirty Hands," 175–76.

35. Ibid., 176–77. See also Max Weber, "Politics as a Vocation," in *From Max Weber: Essays in Sociology*, trans. H. Gerth and C. W. Mills (New York, 1946) 77–128.

36. Tompkins, *West of Everything*, 128.

37. Ibid., 127.

38. Friedrich Nietzsche, *Beyond Good and Evil*, trans. W. Kaufmann (New York, 1966), 201.

39. Ibid., 203.

40. MacIntyre, *After Virtue*, 205.

41. Nietzsche, *Beyond Good and Evil*, 205.

42. Ibid.

43. Ibid.

44. Immanuel Kant, *Lectures on Ethics*, trans. L. Infield (New York, 1963).

45. Ibid.

46. Richard Taylor, "The Virtue of Pride," in *Reflective Wisdom: Richard Taylor on Issues that Matter*, ed. J. Donnelly (Buffalo, N.Y., 1989) chap. 18, 228.

47. Ibid., 229.

48. Kant, *Lectures on Ethics*.

49. Jane Austen, *Pride and Prejudice* (1813, Franklin Center, Pa., 1980), 356.

50. Richard Taylor, "The Virtue of Pride," 228.

51. MacIntyre, *A Short History of Ethics*, 78.

52. Austen, "The Christian Tragic Hero," 54.

53. Gabriele Taylor, *Pride, Shame, and Guilt* (Oxford, 1985), 47.

54. Richard Taylor, "The Virtue of Pride," 232.

55. Ibid., 232.

56. French, *Responsibility Matters*, chap. 5.

57. Gabriele Taylor, *Pride, Shame, and Guilt*, 60.

58. Helen Merrell Lynd, *On Shame and the Search for Identity* (London, 1958), 49.

59. Austen, *Pride and Prejudice*, 309.

60. Gabriele Taylor, *Pride, Shame, and Guilt*, 38.

61. Ibid.

· 5 ·

ARISTOTLE CONTEMPLATING THE DYING DUKE

I

Alasdair MacIntyre has written that in classical heroic societies, like the one described by Homer, a person simply is what that person does. A person and his or her actions are identical. Nothing is hidden.[1] Hermann Frankel, on the same theme, notes that in such cultures "a man . . . makes himself completely and adequately comprehended in [his actions]; he has no hidden depths . . . [The] factual report of what men do and say, everything that men are, is expressed, because they are no more than what they do and say and suffer."[2] From within such a world view, all virtues are manifested only in actions.

The Greek word for virtue, *arete*, in the Homeric epics means excellence in what one does, in one's actions. There is the *arete* of a runner, and even the *arete* of his feet. MacIntyre reminds us that "This concept of virtue or excellence is more alien to us than we are apt at first to recognize. [However], it is not difficult for us to recognize the central place that strength will have in such a conception of human excellence or the way in which courage will be one of the central virtues, perhaps the central virtue."[3]

Little wonder that Aristotle spends so much time in the *Nicomachean Ethics* clarifying the concept of the virtue of courage. In so doing he provides illustrations from the Homeric epics. The westerner's world view—what the westerner cares most about—intersects the Homeric world view in crucial places, some of which I have already mentioned. Suppose then we put to Aristotle another resource for the study of courage. Let him contemplate the dying Duke, John Wayne, playing the part of J. B. Books and (*not* coincidentally) himself and his career, rather than, as Rembrandt would have Aristotle contemplating, "the Bust of Homer."

For Aristotle, true courage must be concerned with facing the most terrible of all evils: death. But not just any kind of death is involved in courage. Aristotle tells us, "What kind of death . . . does bring out courage?

107

Doubtless the noblest kind, and that is death in battle, for in battle a man is faced by the greatest and the most noble of dangers . . . Properly speaking, therefore, we might define as courageous a man who fearlessly faces a noble death."[4]

Only death in noble circumstances, e.g., death in battle!

The typical plot of a Western clearly places its main characters in those "situations that bring a sudden death." The showdown—the gun battle—is a standard climax of Westerns, and, by its very nature, the battle is intended to reveal the true characters of the westerners. But are such gunfights noble circumstances?

It should be recalled that earlier I discussed the scene in *The Shootist* in which Books visits Doctor Hostetler. During that scene he is provided with a rather graphic account of how the cancer in his body will advance and how the pain will increase until he is unable to get out of bed. "One morning you're just going to wake up and say 'Here I am in this bed and here I'm going to stay.' " He is given laudanum to ease the pain, but he is told that after awhile that will prove useless. Then the doctor hints to him that he should consider suicide rather than suffer through the excruciating series of events that the disease has in store for him. The doctor, in fact, leads into that suggestion by remarking that he could not do it in his own case because he does not have Books's courage. Books only grunts as he leaves the office.

We, and especially media reporters, tend to throw words like "courage" and "brave" around with as little care as we talk of tragedy. Having recently watched some of the Olympic Games on television, I am satiated with "tragic" and "courageous." I wonder sometimes whether reporters have any other words in their vocabularies. In one three hour period the television audience was told how courageous a diver was because she was to attempt a difficult dive, how tragic was the failure of a runner to finish a race because she pulled a thigh muscle, and how brave a gymnast must have been to attempt a vault when she was in pain. "Hero," of course, got even more overworked, usually accompanied by some sappy music sung by a lead vocalist and a choir of thousands. However, we typically talk about a person showing courage when he or she has to deal with pain and suffering. If we are ready and willing to talk that way about the healthiest of the specimens of the human race among us: Olympic athletes, it is not surprising that we are willing to talk of the courage of a person suffering from a terminal disease. "He showed great courage in the final stages of the illness." That's what we might say to express our admiration for the way he coped with the pain and suffering he must have been experiencing. But would Aristotle be willing to call such a person courageous?

In a way that is much more persuasive than may first appear to us, Aristotle would insist that a person may face the pain of a terminal illness with a certain admirable toughness, but that that person cannot be courageous with respect to it. Aristotle writes, "In disease the brave man is fearless for he has given up hope, he dislikes the thought of death in this shape . . . We show courage in situations where there is the opportunity of showing prowess or where death is noble; but in the form of death in disease neither of these conditions is fulfilled."[5]

Why would he say this? In part, in situations of terminal illness where the pain ultimately overwhelms the person, there is no real scope for the afflicted to act, no opportunity for prowess. For Aristotle, the scope of the person's actions in the circumstances is always crucial. And, it so happens, this is the central problematic of *The Shootist*. J. B. Books can die the painful death of cancer that the laudanum will not be able to overcome or he can die another death, the death of a gunfighter, a shootist, a death in which he has a genuine opportunity to display his prowess, in which he has a scope of actions in which he can hope to display his virtue. As we are shown in the clips that begin the film, Books has been a courageous person, a town-taming lawman.

What is involved in the expression of the virtue of courage? In the first place and important for Aristotle, courage is an executive virtue. That is, courage is a virtue that is always practiced in the cause of some end that is over and above the expression of courage itself—courage is not practiced only as an end in itself. In effect, unlike some of the other virtues, courage has both an internal and an external goal, to borrow language from David Pears.[5] Its internal goal is the one it shares with other virtues: to be practiced for its own sake. Its external goal will vary from situation to situation, but will be some morally desirable end, or what Aristotle calls "the noble." In the terminal illness case there can be, due to the situation, no external goal, and so courage in such a case cannot serve its executive function. Perhaps we could say that the terminally ill can be courageous in some special or incomplete sense because they can express courage for its own sake, but Aristotle rejects such an account in the *Eudemian Ethics* (1229a), where he calls such a truncated version of courage toughness and not courage at all, just as the *Nicomachean Ethics* lends itself to this reading, as above.

Being tough with respect to his immanent death is not enough for a character like Books. He has been a personification of courage and his life is being cheapened by a noncourageous death, a death that the local buffoon of a marshal (played by Harry Morgan) cannot help pointing out to him is not only ironic, but downright comic.

> Marshal Thibido (to Books): Excuse me if I don't pull a long face. I can't
> . . . Don't take too long to die. Be a gent and convenience everybody
> and do it soon . . . The day they lay you away, what I'll do on your
> grave won't pass for flowers . . . Keeping you alive long enough to die
> natural is costing us a pretty penny . . . How you feelin'? A little more
> poorly everyday? Books, this is nineteen ought one, the old days are
> gone and you don't know it. We got a waterworks, telephones, and
> lights, and we'll have our streetcar electrified by next year, and we've
> started to pave the streets. Oh, we've still got some weedin' to do, but
> once we're rid of people like you, we'll have a goddamn Garden of
> Eden here. To put it in a nutshell, you've outlived your time . . . When
> my time comes to die, I won't drag it out. I'll just do it. Why the hell
> don't you?

A smarmy newspaper reporter, the undertaker, and a golddigging ex-girlfriend provide Books with ample evidence that his life is not coming to an end worthy of the way he has lived, of the virtue he has personified. What he cares most about is being denied him by the disease. Aristotle wrote that "human good turns out to be activity of soul in accordance with virtue . . . 'in a complete life'."[6] Books comes to understand that his plan to die alone in the bed in the boarding house, after he has read the entire newspaper he purchased on arrival in Carson City, does not befit who he is. It offends his character. It does not appropriately conclude his life. To do that he must find a courageous way to die. The lead story in the newspaper is the death of Queen Victoria. Books tells Bond Rogers, the landlady of the boardinghouse:

> Books: Well, maybe she outlived her time. Maybe she was a museum
> piece. But she never lost her dignity, nor sold her guns. She hung onto
> her pride and went out in style. Now that's the kind of an old gal I'd
> like to meet.

Of course, he is comparing her to himself, and he does not like the way he looks in the comparison.

For Aristotle, to be truly courageous a person must face the dangers of the deadly activity "for the sake of the noble, the noble being the end of virtue." What does that mean? The noble is, as already noted, the external goal of courage, but does Aristotle think that squarely facing a deadly activity in itself is noble? Some commentators seem to read him that way. Early in *Welcome to Hard Times*, Henry Fonda's character, Mayor Blue, makes a rational decision not to stand up to the vicious Man from Bodie, played by Aldo Ray. For doing so, he is publicly and privately humiliated and tormented by the prostitute Molly, played by Janice Rule, whom Ray beat and raped. Finally, and despite his better judgment, Fonda does go out, gun in hand, to face the deadly danger, to meet Ray when the latter returns to again wreck the town. He meets the danger, however, in what seems like a less than courageous way. Blue permits a number of other, less capable, townsfolk to try first to stop Ray. All are killed, and only after Ray has emptied his guns, does Fonda kill him. Did he do the noble thing ignobly? Is that courageous? Was just facing the danger sufficient for the act to be noble? It looks more like facing the danger is a necessary, but not a sufficient condition for the act to be courageous. *Welcome to Hard Times* really doesn't explore the issue. It is more concerned with the psychological, and ultimately mortal) costs of hatred than with an examination of courage. (Of some interest may be the fact that the virtues preached throughout the film by Blue are the Christian standards, while Molly rants about the need for revenge, courage, and skill in the use of firearms, a reverse of the usual roles of men and women in Westerns. Blue does have to desert, at the critical moment, his attempt to sustain Christian love and forgiveness in order to kill the rampaging Ray. Then, in a somewhat perverse act, but one motivated by his fury and disgust that he has had to forgo his pacifist commitments in no small measure to please Molly, Blue carries the corpse into her room to show her that her arch-enemy is dead. The young boy Molly has been training to protect her rushes in with a gun and accidentally kills her.)

An alternative interpretation of Aristotle's point would be that an act is noble only if the deadly danger is faced for the sake of a noble object or the noble end to be attained. Such an interpretation better fits with other things Aristotle says about courage. For example, the nobility of the objective of the death-risking activity, the external goal, must be involved, otherwise he would have little reason to exclude cases of facing terminal illness. Courage shares this condition with moral heroism, when nobility is understood in terms of "morally desirable."[7] In other words, unless the external goal of the activity is morally desirable, talk of courage (and heroism) can only be hyperbolic.

Throughout his analysis, Aristotle seems intent on avoiding a confusion of behavior that actually reveals or expresses the virtue of courage with what I have elsewhere called deep play.[8] (I did not coin the term "deep play." I think it is owed to Bentham, but I cannot confirm that.) I define "deep play" as any activity in which the stakes are so high that it is irrational for anyone to engage in it. The marginal utility of what one might gain is far outweighed by the disutility of what one stands to lose.[9] As an example of deep play think of climbing Mount Everest without using supplemental oxygen supplies or surfing the Bonsai Pipeline at the height of the fury of a hurricane. A courageous person does not have what Pears calls "darage," the "virtue," if there were one, that thrillseekers, those who are daring or swashbuckling, display. Pears writes, "Darage is concerned only with desires for a single type of object, risks . . . [T]he man of darage exposes himself to risks medially, but pointlessly."[9] Throughout Westerns, the thrillseeker is mocked and revealed to be someone without virtue. In *Unforgiven*, for example, the Schofield Kid is both literally shortsighted and ultimately incapable of stomaching his violent acts.

Courage and darage can be distinguished because the former, as already noted, essentially has both an internal and an external goal, while, on Pears's account, the latter essentially has only an internal goal. The deep player participates in death-risking activities for the sake of being daring. It is darage for its own sake. Darage, I suppose, sometimes may have a kind of external goal: short-term happiness (it makes me feel good or it is a kick or a rush or something like that), but it does not have varying external goals, or at least it does not have them essentially.

To clarify, the internal goal of the virtue of courage is to be courageous for its own sake. In fact, we should expect to find such an internal goal in the case of every virtue. But courage essentially has a second kind of goal, an external one. That is what makes it essentially an executive virtue. Its external goal may vary from situation to situation, but it must be noble, morally desirable, for Aristotle to pronounce the act courageous in the true sense of the virtue. For Aristotle, the best, the most noble, of the external goals of courage is victory in battle, by which he surely meant the citizen soldier's successful defense of his city.

II

Aristotle provides a typology of what might be called false courage. They are types of character that are sometimes confused with courage and do share some elements with courage, but fail to be examples of what Aristotle calls "true courage," and so courage in the fullest sense. They all lack "the incentive of what is noble." Each type shows up with some regularity in Westerns. The first is a person who behaves bravely to gain honors or to avoid punishment or degradation. Aristotle mentions Hector as an example of this type of courage. Hector enters the battle with Achilles, by Homer's account, primarily because he cannot stand the thought of being degraded before his city. Of course, there are also the laurels to be had should he actually succeed in defeating Achilles, an extremely remote possibility. Homer tells us:

> . . . [H]e [Hector] took counsel with his indomitable soul. He thought: 'If I retire behind the gate and wall, Polydamas will be the first to cast it in my teeth that, in this last night of disaster when the great Achilles came to life, I did not take his advice and order a withdrawal into the city, as I certainly ought to have done. As it is, having sacrificed the army to my own perversity, I could not face my countrymen and the Trojan ladies in their trailing gowns. I could not bear to hear some commoner say: "Hector trusted in his own right arm and lost an army." But it will be said, and then I shall know that it would have been a far better thing for me to stand up to Achilles, and either kill him and come home alive or myself die gloriously in front of Troy.[10]

And so he faces Achilles and is killed.

In *The Shootist* both versions of this type of false courage are displayed. Two town "no-goods" try to kill Books in his room in order to gain the glory of having done so. They are utterly unsuccessful, both are killed by Books. In fact, they try to kill him while he is asleep. One can imagine the two of them firming their resolve for the attempt with visions of the honors they will receive for ridding the town of the famous gunfighter. We, of course, can only guess that it never occurred to them that they are not likely to be proclaimed as courageous heroes when the method of their dispatching of Books is revealed to the public. On the other hand, the town's drunken bully Jay Cobb might well be described as building his courage to face Books in the final saloon shoot-out as a way of avoiding punishment. He is released from jail by Marshal Thibido for the sole purpose of shooting it out with Books.

The second type of false courage, noted by Aristotle, is the "courage of experience." He cites professional soldiers as prime examples. Aristotle tells us, "They have the best insight into the many false alarms which war seems to (bring with it). They give the impression of being courageous, because the others do not know what is happening. Moreover, their experience enables them to be efficient in attack and in defense, for they are capable of using arms and are equipped with the best for offensive as well as defensive purposes."[11] Books and the faro dealer Jack Pulford in *The Shootist* both have this sort of courage. But then, so do Shane and Wilson, Frank in *Once Upon a Time in the West*, Ethan Edwards, Conn Vallian, all of those "Man With No Name" characters of Clint Eastwood's spaghetti Western days, and most of the other gunfighting westerners. For Aristotle these professionals only give the impression of courage.

The third type in Aristotle's catalogue is the identification of a "spirited temper" as courage. The idea is that sometimes people who are enraged or very angry behave in ways that might be indistinguishable from the behavior of someone who is truly courageous. Such a description does not fit many of the westerner heroes, but it does seem to apply to Link Jones of *Man of the West*, William Munny, the Preacher, and most of the characters played by James Stewart in the Anthony Mann Westerns, e.g., *The Naked Spur, Winchester '73, Bend in the River,* and *The Man from Laramie.*

Books's third antagonist in the Metropole saloon is Mike Sweeney, whom Gillom describes as mean and someone who hates Books. That hatred propels his actions in the gunfight as he is able to hit Books twice before he is shot dead by Books. Aristotle does go on to say that "the kind of courage that comes from a spirited temper seems to be the most natural and becomes true courage when choice and purpose are added to it."[12] Choice and purpose are the key to turning the angry into the courageous. What type of purpose? Clearly, a noble or morally desirable external goal. Hatred and anger can be or become moral hatred and moral anger, while vengeance, at least in the world view of the westerner, may, in itself be a morally desirable goal. Whether vengeance should be regarded as a morally desirable goal, however, is a topic for another occasion, though it should be noted that Aristotle, in company with most other moral theorists, did not regard it as such. Aristotle writes, "[A]nger gives men pain and revenge pleasure; and although those who fight for these motives are good fighters, they are not courageous . . . However, they have something which closely resembles courage."[13] Link Jones, William Munny, the Preacher, and the James Stewart characters mentioned above arguably convert their anger into purposes that may include, though not exclusively, vengeance. By doing so, they satisfy Aristotle's conditions for courageous action. Think, for example, of *Bend of the River*, in which the men hired by the character played by James Stewart to transport a shipment of supplies to a community of farmers attack Stewart, beat him to a pulp, and set off with the supplies to sell them at a healthy profit to a mining camp. Stewart, almost demonic with anger and hatred, sets out for revenge, but also to reclaim the wagons for the farmers. To do so he must follow on foot and kill off the thieves. Choice and purpose are clearly added to his anger; courage is the result. How important is it that he has two major purposes: (1) to retrieve the supplies for the farmers who will not survive the winter without them; and (2) to avenge the beating he had received and to kill the character played by Arthur Kennedy, whom he had earlier rescued from hanging, but who had joined the thieves and was, in fact, leading them? Most moralists would applaud the former purpose, but many would be reluctant to accept vengeance as a morally desirable goal. They prefer instead to leave retribution to the state and its system of justice or, in line with the Biblical admonition, "To God."

But despite examples in Westerns of mistaken revenge, such as in *The Ox-Bow Incident*, westerners regard vengeance as a morally appropriate goal. Many, such as Harmonica and Cable Hogue, sustain themselves on their plans for vengeance. Hogue is told by the ersatz preacher Josh to stop focusing his life on the revenge he will get against Taggart and Bowen and that "Vengeance is mine, saith the Lord." He shouts back, "Only if He don't take too long and I can watch." Cable, of course, does not wait for God. In the best tradition of the westerner, he exacts his revenge by humiliating the pair and killing Taggart.

As long as we are focused on Aristotle's account of courage, we will have to look for purposes other than or in addition to vengeance to fill the external goal. Independent of Aristotle, however, a strong case can be made that vengeance is a proper moral goal and that the westerner helps us to appreciate the cogency of that view despite a vast philosophical, legal, and political tradition that argues otherwise. That discussion, however, is best left for another volume.

Aristotle's fourth type of false courage is what might be called the "courage of hope."[14] The idea is that those that have hope of success often behave in ways that look like courage, but, as Aristotle says, "People behave the same way when drunk: drinking makes them optimists. But when things turn out contrary to their expectation they run away."[15] Westerners are unlikely to fall in this category because, by and large, they are not optimists, they are not men of hope. Though it would be remiss not to note that at least some westerners seem to get at least some of their courage from a whiskey bottle. William Munny is a case in point, as are the members of the Wild Bunch.

The fifth and last type of false courage mentioned by Aristotle is the type of apparently courageous behavior that is a product of ignorance, generally ignorance of the real dangers. Perhaps there is no better example of this type than Torrey, the Southern homesteader in *Shane* who believes he can stand up to Wilson.

J. B. Books, the dying Duke, certainly does not have type 1, 4, or 5 of false courage. Though he may be angry about the cancer, it is not fair to say that his actions that culminate in the film's (and, as it happened, in Wayne's career's) climax are motivated primarily by anger. So, the third type can also be excluded. As noted earlier, he most clearly is proud of his professionalism, and so he does have the second type of false courage. If the only motivation he has for the final shoot-out against Carson City's

three best gunfighters and town scourges is a final test of his professionalism, then the act is not one of courage. Whether or not the act is a courageous one must then depend, for Aristotle, on whether all that is involved
is the second type of false courage or whether Books has an appropriate
external goal and, more important, what Pears calls the counter-goal of
courage.[16]

III

A "counter-goal" is what the person wants to avoid, wants not to happen.
The counter-goal of courage is injury and death. Courageous persons are
not death-wishers or masochists. They do not engage in dangerous activity
in order to die or to be wounded. Does Books want to avoid the counter-
goals? That is a good question. He clearly expects to die in the forthcoming
gun battle. He arranges for a tombstone and gives away his possessions,
including a pillow he has used to relieve the pain of sitting. But is expecting
to die in an activity equivalent to wanting to die in it? I don't think it has
to be. In fact, Books does not die from the gunfire of his chosen three
opponents. He kills all three and is then shot in the back by a bartender,
the amateur he hadn't figured on. (Something he had instructed Gillom
never to do.) Still, it is difficult to view the film and not conclude that
Books is arranging his death, arranging it in a way that suits his lifestyle.
The fact that it does not quite work out as he expected does not change
the fact that he does not seem averse to the counter-goals of courage.
However, there is more to Aristotle's analysis of courage.

On Aristotle's account, the person of courage has achieved a mean
between the extremes of feelings of fearfulness (cowardice) and feelings of
over-confidence (rashness). The courageous person has "to weigh the
value and the probability of the external goal against the disvalue and probability of the counter-goal."[17] So there are four judgments the courageous
person must make, and he or she can therefore make four kinds of evaluative mistakes regarding a dangerous activity. Two concern the values and
two, the probabilities.

The person's level of confidence relates to his or her judgments of the
probabilities that the external goal and the counter-goal will occur. If you
are very confident, then you believe that it is highly probable that the
external goal will come about and that the counter-goal will not occur.
The higher you put those probabilities, the more confident you are. The
confident gunfighter, Wilson, for example, believes that it is highly probable that he will outdraw and kill his opponent and that he will not be killed

or even injured. Notice, however, that his confidence leaves unexamined the question of whether the external goal he is pursuing is morally desirable or noble. He can be supremely confident, utterly fearless, without ever examining his judgment that what he is doing is something that ought to be done. Confidence never touches on estimates of the values or disvalues involved. It reflects only probability estimates. The homesteader Torrey is very confident, at least at first, when he goes up against Wilson, and he may well have properly evaluated his external goal as a noble one, but his confidence is misplaced and the nobility of the external goal is irrelevant to the situation. Frank in *Once Upon a Time in the West* faces Harmonica with a great deal of confidence, again misplaced. His judgment of the probabilities, though firmly based on his past experiences, is simply wrong, probably because he does not really know his opponent's abilities, and we read on his face the surprise of discovering that he has badly misjudged the probabilities as he discovers he has been mortally wounded and cannot return his gun to its holster. A similar failure is recorded by Jack Pulford in *The Shootist*.

The emotion on the other end of the spectrum from confidence is fear, or rather fearfulness. Fear also relates to judgments of probabilities, specifically to the probability of the counter-goal occurring, to one's being seriously injured or killed. And fear also relates to the disvalue of the counter-goal. But, like confidence, fear bypasses any judgment as to the value of the external goal of the action.

Three of the four evaluative mistakes in judgment that one can make are covered by the extremes of confidence (rashness) and fearfulness. To make a mistake about the probability that the external goal will be achieved by the action—to give it too high a probability—is overconfidence. To give it too low a probability is a form of fearfulness. The person of courage gives it a probability within a reasonable range. Shane, for example, knows that he has a pretty good chance against Wilson and the Rikers, and he certainly sizes up the situation in Grafton's before positioning himself. How Books rates his chances against the three gunfighters in the Metropole is a matter of question. We know that he expects to die, but does he also expect to kill all three or two of the three or at least one of the three before they get him? Again, he positions himself in a way to keep all three in view and he expects the bully Cobb to make the first move. Which Cobb does. Still, as there is a serious question about what Books took the external goal to be, it is difficult to determine whether he calculated its possibility of occurring within a reasonable range. To make a mistake about the probability that the counter-goal will occur, to wrongly believe that it is extremely likely one will be hurt or killed, is fearfulness. But, by the same token, to misjudge the probability of harm coming to oneself by believing oneself to be invulnerable in the circumstances is most likely extremely rash. The person of courage seeks the medial point, rating the probability of the counter-goal neither too high nor too low.

There can be little issue with mistaking the value of the counter-goal. As it is death or injury, and both are greatly disvalued with respect to what the westerner cares about, they are to be avoided or postponed as long as possible. This does cause a problem in *The Shootist*, however, where Books is dying a painful death that he does not want to endure because it will diminish his self-worth, while a death that occurs in a glorious gun battle would be more in keeping with his lifestyle. We well may wonder whether types of deaths should not receive rather different values. In other words, perhaps there is a scale of disvalue of the counter-goal in which death of one type is lower on the scale than death of another type. Books is choosing a death with a lesser disvalue to him than the one the doctor described. This is all true to the story, but it does not help us to determine whether or not Books's final actions were courageous. It is surely the case that he would have preferred to live rather than die any kind of death. His choice of a death that he regards as more befitting who he has been in life may, in fact, be admirable, but, again, it is still not clear that it was courageous. The fact that it is different from the noncourageous death in bed from cancer, does not in itself make it courageous. Nor does the fact that he chose it while the other was visited on him.

It is unclear from Aristotle's scheme how the value of the external goal is related to judgments made under the influence of either of the extreme feelings of which courage is the mean. In fact, the whole Aristotelian structure in which the virtue of courage is medial between rashness and fearfulness (cowardliness) assumes that the person of courage has weighed the value of the external goal against the disvalue of the counter-goal, though a mistake in such an evaluation is not necessarily to be rash or fearful. A rash person, such as Torrey in *Shane*, may have underestimated the probability of the harm that will come to him and/or the probability that he will rid the valley of the gunfighter Wilson, and/or the disvalue of the counter-goal that will occur: his death. But over- or underestimating the value of the external goal—ridding the valley of the gunfighter—would not make him rash. Simply, there is no necessary link between overconfidence and overestimating the value of the external goal. Still, to be courageous one must properly evaluate the external goal.

IV

The courageous person, on Aristotle's account, is not fearless. He says, "The man, then, who faces and who fears the right things and from the right motive, in the right way and at the right time, and who feels confidence under the corresponding conditions, is brave; for the brave man feels and acts according to the merits of the case . . ."[18] The courageous person fears what is fearful. For example, he or she does not lose his or her fear of dying or of serious injury. Shane may not be afraid to die, but he fears dying. Books certainly fears dying. That fear, the fear of sudden death, rides with all westerners. However, the courageous person takes the risk for the sake of the external goal and so he or she appears to be fearless when he or she acts. As Tompkins writes, "Once you no longer believe you are eternal spirit, risking your life becomes the supreme form of heroism, the bravest thing a person can do . . . The Western plot . . . turns . . . on external conflicts in which men prove their courage to themselves and to the world by facing their own annihilation."[19]

As Pears makes clear and Aristotle does not, there must be two levels in the acts of the courageous person. At one level, what we might call the stage of planning, after J. L. Austin's discussion of the machinery of action,[20] emotions enter in and the courageous person is fearful. He or she wants to avoid death or injury, courage's counter-goal. But by the stage of execution, he or she is fearless. At either the decision or the resolve stage in Austin's machinery, he or she has hardened his or her heart to the task at hand, taking, what Pears calls, "an all things considered" approach to what needs to be done to realize the external goal. Still, it is not to be forgotten that on Aristotle's account, the estimation of the value of that external goal, and especially mistakes relative to that estimation never fall into the category of rashness or fearfulness. They are based on one's conception of what is morally desirable in the circumstances and that can be seriously, perhaps fatally, skewed by bad intelligence or by a failure of appreciation, two other stages in Austin's conception of the machinery of action.

For Aristotle, as previously noted, the courageous person avoids the extremes of cowardice (fearfulness) and extreme confidence (rashness). Courage is the mean. However, according to Sir David Ross[21], Aristotle is wrong in his analyses of the virtues, including courage, because, Ross believes, Aristotle failed to grasp that all virtue is self-control. Had Aristotle understood that all virtue is self-control, Ross thinks he would have seen that there are two pairs of extreme reactions of people to dangerous situations. He writes, "There is not only a tendency to avoid danger, but a tendency to rush into it—a tendency less common than the other, but one which exists and which no less than the other must be mastered 'for the sake of the noble.' One soldier must not be a slave of his 'cheer,' as this tendency has been called, any more than another should be the slave of his fear."[22] Ross argues that there are two different corresponding virtues, not one. The idea is something like this: you get the feeling, the vice is to give in, the virtue is to resist, to show self-control. Ross's version lines up the triads as follows:

1.] FEELING = Fear / VIRTUE = Courage / VICE = Cowardice
2.] FEELING = Love of Danger / VIRTUE = Discretion / VICE = Rashness·

On Ross's account then, Aristotle should have noticed that there are two different virtues, courage and discretion, not one in which courage is the mean between cowardice and rashness. And, as he reminds us, "internally courage is quite a different thing from discretion."[23]

I agree with Pears that Ross, not Aristotle, is wrong. Aristotle, rightly, sees that the scale with respect to danger runs from excessive fear to fearlessness and that there can only be a single medial point on that scale. There are not two distinct scales. "It makes no difference to the nature of this virtue that one person may find it hard to achieve because he tends to deficiency, and another because he tends to excess."[24]

Also, Ross gets Aristotle wrong on the object of fear, the counter-goal of courage. It is not danger, but injury and, ultimately, death that is feared by the courageous person. If danger were what is feared or toward which one is attracted, then courage would disintegrate into darage. Only masochists seek self-harm, some people are rather attracted to danger.

Still, the external goal of courage is crucial. Its value must be weighed by the person against the disvalue of the harm to that person that is likely to result. Here, it seems to me, we get into the most serious disagreements about whether or not a person is courageous. Suppose that the person incorrectly values the external goal. It really is not noble. It is not a morally desirable thing to achieve. It is morally flawed, even wicked. Can a person exhibit courage in pursuit of such a goal? I think Aristotle would agree with me that such a person cannot do so. A soldier fighting for an immoral cause, regardless of whether he believes that cause to be right and just, cannot be morally courageous, though he may be tough and the like, and he certainly may be daring. Wilson is not courageous. Nor is Frank. But is Books?

Books learns of three "scourges" on the community, all of whom have reputations as gunfighters, and he invites all three to meet him for a drink at the Metropole in celebration of his birthday. He knows full well that none of them can resist the temptation to enhance his reputation by killing the famous J. B. Books. And he heads out to meet them. He is told by Bond Rogers before he starts out for the Metropole that Carson City is experiencing a false spring. It is January, but there is a look and feel of

April, a new beginning, in the air. It is a deception, for winter and death are the reality. Still, the shootout offers Books a false spring, a glorious way to overcome the wintry death from cancer he has decided not to allow himself to endure. Still, it is a false spring, for it will be death and not life.

In the gunfight, quite remarkably and despite receiving a number of gunshot wounds, Books kills all three of his chosen antagonists while avoiding a mortal wound. The bartender enters with a shotgun and shoots him in the back. Gillom, who witnesses the bartender's act, takes Books's gun and shoots the bartender three times, killing him, before Books dies. Did Books die a death with courage or a death with darage? Was it just a reckless form of deep play that has no particular virtue and indeed may well have been a self-indulgent vice? The film is ambiguous with respect to the information that would help us decide the answers to such questions. If Books's sole reason for bringing the three other gunfighters to the saloon that false spring morning was to engineer for himself a death that would be faster, less painful, and more in keeping with his personal image, the act is not one of courage by Aristotle's account. It is merely an elaborate form of assisted suicide. But if his primary reason for the saloon gunfight was to rid the town of three undesirable scourges, in much the manner he had, during his career as a marshal, rid other towns of similar threats to the future of civilized progress, then that external goal might well be regarded as noble and the act, one of courage. With respect to the latter interpretation we do have his conversations with Marshal Thibido about the need to pull a few weeds before Carson City could become "a goddamn Garden of Eden." That Books would never have wanted to live in a garden, much less the Garden of Eden, is irrelevant. Such is the plight of all of the westerner heroes, and especially John Wayne's characters. It is instructive that under the opening credits we are shown clips from some of Wayne's Westerns, from *Red River* to *El Dorado*. His first major **role**, of course, was as the Ringo Kid in *Stagecoach*. That film concludes with the Ringo Kid riding out of town with the prostitute Dallas to, in the doctor's words "escape civilization." While in *Rio Bravo*, Wayne as the sheriff unambiguously defends the town and law and order courageously. Although the clips are ostensibly to provide us with a survey of Books's career, they are also a survey of Wayne's career, a career that highlighted the tensions the westerner hero faces between his consuming desire to escape civilization's relentless march over the wilderness and his need to sustain his honor by courageously using his skills in a noble cause. Unfortunately (or ironically) for the westerner, the occasions to do the latter almost invariably involve him in aiding and abetting that from which he most desires to escape, civilization. If sustaining his honor by using his skills in a noble cause is what Books sees himself as doing, he is not only doing Carson City a favor, he could be doing something courageous, even heroic.

V

Truly heroic acts, at least from the moral point of view, like acts that Aristotle would regard as examples of true courage, must be done in order to achieve morally desirable ends. Truly heroic acts must have noble external goals and should also be undertaken with full knowledge that one's life and/or what one cares most about is at risk of loss. There is no such thing as accidental moral heroism. This condition of self-sacrifice is noted by a number of philosophers, including John Rawls who identifies heroic deeds as good acts that would be moral obligations except for the cost run by the hero.[25] Heroic deeds, then, are nonobligatory actions involving extraordinary risks to those doing them. We should also expect that a hero had appropriate moral intentions when he or she undertook the deed. Usually the hero will intend to benefit others. So heroism is typically altruistic. Books may be benefiting the good citizens of Carson City, but that can only be a secondarily intended outcome of his actions, if he intended it at all. As he cannot possibly be sure that he will succeed in killing off the three gunfighters before he is killed by one of them, it could only be a rather remote intention at best.

In his famous paper "Saints and Heroes,"[26] J. O. Urmson noted that typically in moral philosophy actions are classed in three, supposedly exhaustive, categories. Some acts are obligatory, some are of no concern to morality, while the remainder are forbidden. Kant wrote that the moral law (the categorical imperative) asserts an obligation that "either commands or prohibits; it sets forth as a duty the commission or omission of an action. An act that is neither commanded nor forbidden is merely permissible, since there is no law to limit one's freedom (moral title) to perform it, and so no duty with regard to the action. An action of this kind is called morally indifferent."[27] Heroic deeds are "permissible" but they do not seem to be morally indifferent. "Hero" is surely a term of favorable moral evaluation. Indeed, it is a term of high praise. But if heroic deeds are not obligatory, where do they fit in the threefold classification?

If Shane had a moral obligation to face Wilson and the Rikers, we should regard him as a moral coward, a shirker, had he not done so and not a hero because he did. But if he is a hero, then what he did was "merely permissible" in Kant's terms, and morality should be indifferent to it. But then why should he be held in so high a regard for his action? On the other hand, if we are not morally indifferent to heroism and we do not forbid it (as we do not), then it should be subsumed into moral obligation. If that were the case, however, all of us could be obligated at least on some occasions to act heroically, and such actions would take a great deal of the shine off heroism. The old threefold categorization of actions for moral evaluative purposes might be generally inadequate and in need of serious modification.

One way to affect such a modification might be to adopt Kant's distinction between types of duties.[28] Perfect duties are negative duties— duties of omission, for example, duties not to commit suicide, not to act out of carnal lust, not to lie, etc. We are always, Kant argued, morally constrained with respect to these duties. To transgress them is vice. Imperfect duties, on the other hand, for Kant, are duties of virtue. They go beyond the formal principles of action and require the adoption of a purpose, not just the performing or the refraining from specific actions. There is considerable room for choice in determining the actions one will take to meet the required end and when one will meet them. If there is a moral law commanding us to make as one of our ends the benefiting of others, it will not be violated if we do not benefit others on any specific occasion when we had the opportunity. You do not have to give to every beggar who approaches you with hand held out. As one gets older, if one is to meet one's obligation to perform this duty, the opportunities one has to refuse the beggar become fewer and fewer. If one has not yet met one's imperfect duties as one approaches death, it would be virtually impossible to distinguish them from perfect duties. You have got to get them done. There is also the matter of luck in meeting up with occasions to perform imperfect duties. Should a person who, owing to the sheltered nature of his or her existence, has never had the opportunity, seek out objects of charity, go looking for beggars? Is that then a perfect moral duty?

Benevolence looks like a Kantian imperfect duty of virtue that can be met with occasional charitable donations. What Shane did for the Starretts and the other homesteaders would also seem to satisfy the benevolence duty, but intuitively there is a vast moral difference between giving a donation to the needy and risking one's life to face a gunfighter like Wilson. Only the latter would seem to qualify as heroic. Furthermore, Kant noted that "To provide oneself with such comforts as are necessary merely to enjoy life . . . is a duty to oneself . . . How far should we expend our means in practicing benevolence? Surely not to the extent that we ourselves would finally come to need the charity of others."[29] Heroism, however, requires one to put one's life, or what one deeply cares about, at risk, and if anything, that requirement violates one of Kant's perfect duties to oneself: "The first of man's duties to himself as an animal being is to preserve himself in his animal nature."[30]

In the Casuistical Questions related to his examination of this perfect duty, Kant asked, "Is it murder to hurl oneself to certain death (like Curtius) in order to save one's country?—or is voluntary martyrdom, offering oneself as a sacrifice for the welfare of the whole human race, also to be considered an act of heroism?"[31] Unfortunately, Kant never answers his questions, nor does he, at least in this case, indicate how the answer should go. He seems to hold heroism in high moral regard, but not as a higher obligation than the preservation of oneself.

In Kant's analysis, apparent conflicts between the perfect duty to preserve one's life and the performing of an act of heroism that risks that life, or what one regards as the quality of that life, for the purpose of benefiting others may arise because they are the products of two different grounds of obligation. Kant maintained, however, that not the stronger obligation, but the stronger ground of obligation takes precedence, resolving the apparent conflict. For Kant, the ground of the obligation of self-preservation, apparently, is stronger than benevolence. Kant's own "casuistical" questions cast doubt, however, on whether it is so in all heroic cases. In any event, he tells us that failure to meet a perfect duty, such as self-preservation, is vice and guilt, while not meeting an imperfect duty is "mere lack of moral worth," "want of virtue," "lack of moral strength."

It seems fair to Kant to say that Shane has no moral obligation to face Wilson and the Rikers, though it may be one way he has of achieving an end that is an imperfect duty. That end, however, is, arguably at least, not superior to his perfect duty of self-preservation, the transgression of which surely is risked by the showdown in Grafton's.

The traditional utilitarians offer a simpler answer than Kant to the question of the moral status of heroic acts. For them, if it is the only action in the circumstances that conforms to the principle of utility, it is the only morally right thing to do. One, therefore, has a moral obligation to do it regardless of whether one is likely to lose limb or life in doing it. Still further, it would seem that if there are two or more actions that conform, to varying degrees, to the principle of utility, that is, they maximize general utility to a greater or lesser extent, then the action that increases general utility to the greater extent, with things being more or less equal, is a moral obligation. Westerners like Shane, the Preacher, Tom Doniphon, and John Russell, despite their personal risk-taking, on a utilitarian account, may be doing no more than what they have moral obligations to do in the circumstances in which they find themselves. For a utilitarian there may be times in which by doing what you ought, you suffer. You might even die. It has been said that the duties of life are sometimes greater than life.

In *Hombre*, John Russell gives the impression that he accepts some-thing like the utilitarian conclusion when he takes on the task of saving Mrs. Favor, though he does not seem to accept the utilitarian argument. He sees the task as his moral duty because he is the only member of the group with the skills that could conceivably lead to success. Shane makes a similar argument to Joe and Marion Starrett. A modified version of the position that there is a duty to be heroic would be that heroism is a duty for those who can be heroic. Capacity determines duty. If you can, but you don't, you're guilty of moral failure. Still, the stakes in heroism are often life and death. How can heroic actions be another set of obligations, just because you have the ability and the opportunity?

Urmson argues that morality has two realms: that of what must be done or avoided, the realm of obligation, and a higher realm where we can evaluate actions as good and commend them to others, but where the morality is one of aspiration, not requirement. The idea of two moral realms is useful if we understand that the high praise we extend to heroic persons like Shane does not commit us to saying that we have obligations to act in ways exactly similar to them or that they had obligations to act as they did. Instead, moral praise in such cases points at the virtue—the integrity—manifested by some of the westerner heroes.

Westerners like Shane, Conn Vallian, John Russell, Will Kane, Tom Doniphon, Conagher, and Hondo Lane seem to have predominantly altru-istic intentions as they knowingly risk their lives. Clearly, some of them have very complex motives of which the altruistic one is only a part of the complex, but a number of westerners do not succeed in any way to satisfy the altruistic condition of heroism. For example, Harmonica, Ethan Ed-wards, and William Munny are hardly altruistic. The Preacher may be in-terested to some degree in answering Megan's prayer, but we learn that his dominant reason for going to town to take on Stockburn's posse is that they are responsible for killing him in his previous incarnation. It is an old score that needs to be settled. The benefit to the independent miners seems to be almost a happy second effect. Ethan Edwards is consumed with ven-geance, as is Harmonica. Whatever benefits their violent actions may con-fer on others is of little interest to them.

But what is so important about altruism? There is a conceit in moral philosophy that favors impartial altruism. Many Westerns challenge that conceit. If all that is really important is that the act be done to bring about noble or morally desirable ends, then impartial altruism may be just one desirable type of end among others. It might not be close to the most important or most desirable end or most noble end, morally speaking. Ven-geance may be a higher or more noble end.

I realize that such a claim requires considerable argument and, as noted above, I will postpone the attempt to make the case to a subsequent work. Let it suffice here merely to remain the suggestion that, if vengeance can be persuasively shown to be a morally desirable end, then Ethan Edwards, William Munny, Harmonica, and those near-demonic characters James Stewart played in his 1950s Westerns not only are truly courageous, but they are heroic. In fact, Pike Bishop, Dutch, and the Gorch brothers of *The Wild Bunch* would also be heroic when, at the end of the film, they avenge the torture and death of Angel by taking on General Mapache's army, though there is virtually nothing altruistic about their actions.

But what of J. B. Books? He is not avenging anything. He has barely met Cobb, and it is Sweeney who has a reason to seek revenge against him, not the other way around. He and Pulford know each other only by reputation. So if Books's final shoot-out is more than deep play, either we must be persuaded that he is trying to benefit the people of Carson City in the way previously suggested or he has some other morally desirable, noble external goal in mind. Perhaps he is trying to protect his own integrity. Would that count?

VI

"Integrity," as I use the term, refers to a particular virtue, not to a combination or culmination of all virtues or a significant number of them. Admittedly, on a not unreasonable account, integrity might be treated as a kind of conglomerate virtue, one that unites the other virtues or even supervenes on the existence in a person of the other, or a significant number of the other, virtues. If that were the case, we would say that someone has integrity if he or she is just courageous, temperate, trustworthy, etc. However, integrity is more often understood as independent of the possession of the other virtues, in fact, as something a person might have while lacking some or all of the other virtues.

Admittedly, there are etymological reasons to see integrity as a unifier, if not of other virtues, then as a unifier of various aspects of a person's character. After all, the first entry for the term in *The Oxford English Dictionary* is "The condition of having no part or element taken away or wanting; undivided or unbroken state; material wholeness, completeness, entirely."[32] "Integrity" shares roots with "intact" and "integer," suggesting a unity or a whole. Gabriele Taylor reminds us that a person of integrity is typically thought to be someone "whose self is whole and integrated."[33] But a whole composed of what? What is integrated?

Martin Benjamin points out that like many moral concepts, integrity can be clarified by looking at ways people are said to lack it.[34] He characterizes six types of people who may be said to lack integrity: the moral chameleon, the opportunist, the hypocrite, the self-deceiver, the weak-willed, and those coerced into violating their convictions. Suffice it to say that people can be traitors to their own integrity in myriad subtle ways and in degrees and combinations of the various types.[35]

The lesson Benjamin would have us learn from even a cursory examination of these types is that when we talk about someone having integrity we are referring in some way, albeit obliquely, to a wholeness or a unity characterizable as an integration of what that person actually values with what he or she says and does. Benjamin refers to integrity as "an integrated triad consisting of (1) a reasonably coherent and relatively stable set of highly cherished values and principles (2) verbal behavior expressing these values and principles and (3) conduct embodying one's values and principles and consistent with what one says.[36]

This account of integrity, of course, is purely structural and formalistic. In fact, Rawls[37] and Flanagan[38] class integrity as a virtue of form, a structural virtue, and oppose it to contentful virtues. Flanagan writes, "[It] *(a virtue like integrity)* tell[s] us that a life possesses certain internal goods. But [it] do[es] not tell us enough about the quality of a person's projects and convictions or about the actual historical connections his life has with the lives of others with whom he interacts—others who may be permitted to make certain demands of him."[39] For Flanagan, a person can lose his or her integrity, while holding "onto the projects with which he [or she] most identifies and thus not be alienated," because integrity "is a matter of possessing the ability to act on what one recognizes as the most important reasons for actions even if these reasons conflict with other reasons."[40]

The "integrity formalism" of Benjamin, Rawls, and Flanagan allows that someone has integrity, regardless of the content of his or her commitments, as long as he or she believes that he or she is acting on his or her most important reasons for action when they conflict with other reasons he or she has for acting, as long as there is an integration of his or her values, his or her words, and his or her deeds. It is easy to see how Books would satisfy this formal criteria, and how he preserves his integrity by arranging the showdown at the Metropole. Such a formalism, though it can account for the difference between a person of integrity and a chameleon, an opportunist, a hypocrite, or a self-deceiver, fails importantly to distinguish between the person of integrity and the person with deeply or strongly held unethical or immoral convictions. On the formalist's account, persons with utterly immoral values and principles, those committed to values and principles that motivate actions that are inconsistent with morally desirable or noble goals, can still be properly described as persons of integrity. Stockburn in *Pale Rider,* Frank in *Once Upon a Time in the West,* Liberty Valance and Grimes in *Hombre* all would satisfy the conditions of the integrity formalist.

Surely there should be some moral restrictions on the commitments one can have, if one is to be credited with possessing a virtue. In *The Wild Bunch,* Pike and Dutch have the following conversation:

> Pike: What would you do in his place? He gave his word.
> Dutch: Gave his word to a railroad!
> Pike: It's his word.
> Dutch: That ain't what counts. It's who you give it to.

As Mark Halfon writes: "One desirable consequence . . . of embracing the view that persons of integrity are typically true to their commitments is that it allows for such persons to embrace a diversity of ideals or principles and may help to create an air of toleration."[41] Even if we grant that, there is something rather morally unsavory about holding someone in high regard not because he or she has admirable principles, but because he or she has, in Taylor's words, "the courage of his [or her] convictions"?[42]

The formalist account is inadequate, if only because it almost completely excludes the virtuous element of the virtue. Still, the account of integrity that sits on the other side of the spectrum, the one that requires a person of integrity to have only morally justifiable convictions, also has serious problems. For example, on what theory of morality are the convictions of a person of integrity to be tested? If it matters which theory is chosen, then someone could hold and act on convictions that satisfy a generally recognized moral theory, but not the favored one and fail to be a person of integrity. In order to become a person of integrity, that person would have to reject his or her own moral principles. But how then could such a person be regarded as having integrity? Something between the extremes of formalism and designated content must be closer to capturing what we mean by the virtue of integrity. Halfon puts it nicely when he writes, "Persons of integrity must be permitted to cultivate Promethean impulses without being allowed to indulge Procrustean sensibilities."[43]

An alteration to the formalistic account of integrity that should correct its lack of sufficient moral content while not dictating the preferred moral theory could focus on the intentions of the person with respect to the convictions on which he or she is acting, what he or she cares about.

Perhaps what most disturbs us about crediting persons with integrity because they steadfastly pursue obviously wicked courses of action to which they are deeply committed is that most such persons also seem to adamantly refuse to submit their cares, convictions, and beliefs either to the test of truth or to serious moral scrutiny. In short, to be a person of integrity, on this modified account, one must not only believe that one's convictions, what one most cares about, are true and moral (or noble) and one's principles right, one must be in a certain state of mind: one must have the intentions to pursue the issue of whether or not they are true and whether or not they are morally justifiable or noble.

Saying that a person of integrity must intend to pursue the truth of his or her convictions, those on which commitments and cares are based, does not mean that he or she has uncovered the truth or that he or she should not continue to act on those convictions until he or she has uncovered the truth. The intention in question is to pursue their truth and to desert them if they prove to be false. By the same token, a person of integrity must intend to hold or pursue only morally desirable principles and convictions. This does not entail that such a person may not have misguided or downright bad principles or morally undesirable convictions. The crucial difference between this position and integrity formalism is that the person of integrity is required to have a specific set of intentions: the intentions to care about the right sorts of things, i.e., to pursue morally desirable principles and the truth of one's convictions.

Suppose someone proposed that Frank exhibits integrity, but that it is just of an especially unsavory sort. He is a killer, a deceiver, a criminal on a variety of counts. He is, clearly, a revolting sort of person who is all the more villainous because he is so deeply committed to his convictions and the extreme egotism that motivates him. If we say that he has integrity as such a villain, it seems to be, as Peter Winch has written, "an additional count against him, not a point in his favor."[44] We should say instead, however, that the only way Frank could be exhibiting integrity would be if he were actively pursuing the truth of the convictions he holds, and if he had the intention to pursue only morally desirable or noble principles or convictions and was actively trying to determine if he was, in fact, doing that. Frank, of course, has no such intentions. He is hardly a man of integrity. At the very least, he is morally negligent, in just those matters where he ought to be diligent. He ought not to be admitted into the class of those displaying integrity, though the formalist must admit him. In *Shane*, Chris Calloway, the character played by Ben Johnson, does, apparently, have the appropriate intentions. When he realizes he has sided with villains, he quits the Rikers and warns Shane about what Wilson and the Rikers have planned at Grafton's for Joe Starrett.

This is not a contentful account of integrity. Halfon writes, "Persons of integrity sometimes perform ill-advised actions or pursue unjust principles as a result of ignorance, deception, naiveté but ignorance or deception or naiveté by themselves will not bring about a loss of integrity."[45] The intention to pursue the truth and the moral justifiability of one's convictions and principles does not ensure that one will in fact have morally desirable or noble convictions and principles. It ensures that one does not abandon the pursuit for reasons of expediency, and it ensures that one will not intentionally adopt false or immoral convictions and principles. Persons of integrity must at least intend to do what they believe is right in every circumstance and be willing to expose their conception of what is right to serious self- and external examination. Such a view of integrity shackles the formalist's position with the sort of restrictions that should bring it more in line with common intuitions about integrity as a virtue.

Halfon cashes out these restrictions in the following helpful way: "[P]ersons who have integrity . . . do not embrace an undemanding moral point of view. They do not allow prudential considerations to outweigh moral commitments. They do not compromise their ideals or principles in the face of adversity. Instead, they embrace a moral point of view that urges them to be conceptually clear, logically consistent, apprised of relevant empirical evidence, and careful about acknowledging as well as weighing relevant moral considerations."[46]

Is J. B. Books such a person? I think the primary point of the film is to demonstrate to us that he is. He certainly does not embrace an undemanding moral point of view. We hear his moral creed twice in the film, at the beginning and when he is giving Gillom a shooting lesson. "I won't be wronged. I won't be insulted, and I won't be laid a hand on. I don't do these things to other people, and I require the same from them." As the film opens we see the way he adheres to his creed. He is accosted by a robber and forced to hand over his wallet. As he does so he pulls a gun and shoots the robber in the stomach.

> Robber: You done murdered me.
> Books: No, but you're going to have a long winter bellyache, you boob.
> Give me that wallet . . . Just the wallet.
> Robber: I can hardly move. You done shot a hole in my stomach. (*He gives Books back his wallet.*)
> Books: I appreciate that.
> Robber: You ain't gonna leave me here?
> Books: Well, it's quite obvious that's what you were gonna do to me.
> Get out of the way. (*Shoves him into a puddle.*) Mister, you better find yourself another line of work. This one sure don't fit your pistol.

Books never seems to let prudential considerations outweigh what he takes to be his moral commitments, his duty. Though he is unforgiving of others, he is equally unforgiving of himself. He relentlessly faces the facts and does not compromise. These are undoubtedly admirable qualities, but conjoined with his earned reputation as a gunfighter, he is increasingly difficult for the Christian Mrs. Rogers to deal with. She recognizes his dignity and his integrity and honors his pride, but he remains a killer in her eyes. Her conversations with him, usually, until the final two days, terminate in arguments or frustrated silence, but they reveal a growing appreciation for his moral worth.

> Mrs. Rogers: Mr. Books, you are a notorious individual, utterly lacking in character or decency. You are an assassin.
> Books: It's according to which end of the gun you're on.
> . . .
> Books: In general, I've had a hell of a good time . . . Bond, I don't believe I ever killed a man who didn't deserve it.
> Mrs. Rogers: Surely, only the Lord can judge that.
> . . .
> Books: Bond, I'm tired of people pawin' over my death for this reason or that or for any reason. A man's death, well, it's about the most private thing in his life . . . It's mine.
> Mrs. Rogers: I suppose it's true of your soul, too?
> Books: My soul is what I've already made of it. You reprimand me for making judgments with a gun barrel poked in my face, but it's all right for you to judge me on hearsay.
> Mrs. Rogers: But the hearsay fits.
> Books: Maybe I'm better than you've already decided . . .
> Mrs. Rogers: Or maybe you just like being a gunman or I suppose you prefer the word "shootist."
> Books: I don't think of myself as either.
> Mrs. Rogers: Oh no, you're some godlike creature of infinite knowledge, aren't you?
> Books: I'm a dying man, scared of the dark.
> Mrs. Rogers: Damn you. Damn you for the pain you've brought into this house.

The pain, of course, is her pain because she realizes that she has misjudged him. He is not a man lacking in character or decency. He is also a man of dignity, as he insists to his ex-girlfriend, and he will hang onto his pride and, like Queen Victoria, go out in style. Books has integrity, right to the end.

It is fair to Books to say that in his final acts he preserves his integrity, his pride, and his dignity, despite the fact that he cannot satisfy the Aristotelian conditions for true courage. I wonder, however, if what he told Mrs. Rogers about everyone he ever killed deserving to die remains true after the shoot-out in the Metropole. None of his three antagonists has, as far as we have seen, committed a crime worthy of death. But then, has Books? On the other hand, perhaps as William Munny tells Little Bill as he shoots him in *Unforgiven,* "Deserves got nothin' to do with it."

NOTES

1. MacIntyre, *After Virtue,* 122.
2. Hermann Frankel, *Early Greek Poetry and Philosophy,* trans. Hadas and Willis (New York, 1973), 79.
3. MacIntyre, *After Virtue,* 122.
4. Aristotle *Nicomachean Ethics,* bk 3, 1115a.
5. David Pears, "Aristotle's Analysis of Courage," in *Midwest Studies in Philosophy* 3 (1978): 273–85.
6. Aristotle *Nicomachean Ethics,* bk 3, 1115b.
7. Ibid., bk 1, 1098a.
8. Peter French, *Responsibility Matters,* chap. 11.
9. Ibid., 114–15.
10. Pears, "Aristotle's Analysis of Courage," 277.
11. Homer, *The Iliad,* 399–400.
12. Aristotle, *Nicomachean Ethics,* 1116b.
13. Ibid., 1117a.
14. Ibid.
15. Ibid.
16. Pears, "Aristotle's Analysis of Courage," 274.
17. Ibid.
18. Aristotle, *Nicomachean Ethics,* 1115b.
19. Tompkins, *West of Everything,* 31.
20. Austin, *Philosophical Papers,* 193–94.
21. David Ross, *Aristotle* (London, 1923), 204–7.
22. Ibid., 206.
23. Ibid.
24. Pears, "Aristotle's Analysis of Courage," 278.
25. John Rawls, *A Theory of Justice* (Cambridge, Mass., 1971), 117.
26. J.O. Urmson, "Saints and Heroes," in *Essays in Moral Philosophy,* ed. A.I. Melden (Seattle, Wash., 1958), 198–216.
27. Immanuel Kant, *The Doctrine of Virtue,* trans. M. Gregor (Philadelphia, Pa., 1964), 21–22.
28. Ibid., 79f.
29. Ibid., 120.

30. Ibid., 84.

31. Ibid., 86.

32. *Oxford English Dictionary* (Oxford, 1971), 1455.

33. Gabriele Taylor, "Integrity," *Proceedings of the Aristotelian Society, Supplementary Volume* 55 (1981): 143.

34. Martin Benjamin, *Splitting the Difference.*

35. The moral chameleon is "anxious to accommodate others and temperamentally indisposed to moral controversy and disagreement. The moral chameleon is quick to modify or abandon previously avowed principles in order to placate others." Moral chameleons have no core set of values for which they stand. They bend to any and all social pressures. They will betray others they only yesterday befriended. When we say of the chameleon that he has no integrity, we mean that he stands by nothing he says or does from day to day, minute to minute. You cannot depend on him because he has committed himself to no core set of values. An opportunist's values and principles are fluid, resembling the chameleon, but the major difference is the opportunist's motive remains personal aggrandizement. "Opportunists will alter their beliefs and behavior whenever they think it will lead to personal gain or advancement."
Hypocrites have one set of values for public display and another that they keep hidden, but are what actually motivates their behavior. Benjamin notes that a deeper understanding of the hypocrite, despite this apparent inconsistency between words and deeds, will reveal "a coherent internal rationale. Underlying the hypocrite's apparent external inconsistencies, then, is a deceitful internal unity . . . Self-deceivers are often motivated by a discrepancy between the values and principles that they like to think of themselves as acting upon and their conduct that is motivated by quite different, incompatible interests and desires. To resolve this tension and, at the same time, to preserve the idealized self-conception while indulging the incompatible interests and desires, they deceive themselves about what they are in fact doing." Self-deceivers think they are internally consistent and positively brimming over with integrity, but it is all a sham. The weak-willed lack the "courage of their convictions," while those coerced into acting against their principles and values generally lack an internal integrity needed to stand up against the coercion. Ibid., 47–51.

36. Ibid., 51.

37. John Rawls, *A Theory of Justice*, 519.

38. Owen Flanagan, *Varieties of Moral Personality* (Cambridge, Mass., 1991).

39. Ibid., 91.

40. Ibid., 92.

41. Mark Halfon, *Integrity* (Philadelphia, 1989), 29–30.

42. Gabriele Taylor, "Integrity," 143.

43. Halfon, *Integrity*, 32.

44. Peter Winch, *Ethics and Action* (London, 1972), 71.

45. Halfon, *Integrity*, 35.

46. Ibid., 36–37.

· 6 ·

The Death of Death

I

The following conversation between Captain Woodrow Call and Pea Eye Parker occurs in *Streets of Laredo* after they come across the old-timer Ben Lilly, whose dogs have been burned by the sadistic Mox Mox.

Call: Damn few left like him.
Pea Eye: Like him how, Captain?
Call: Like him, like Gus, like Hickok, old Kit Carson. They done what they wanted. They went where they wanted. It wasn't always good, but least they lived free lives. You're a farmer yourself, corporal. You're respectable. Charlie Goodnight's got his ranch. It's just the killers and a few like old Ben Lilly that's kept the old ways.
Pea Eye: And you, captain.
Call: What?
Pea Eye: You've kept to the old ways.
Call gives a double take and sighs. Then he stares off to the horizon.

The Man Who Shot Liberty Valance is an especially disturbing film for fans of John Ford. Ford Westerns were typically shot in the broad and spectacular vistas of Monument Valley. The grandeur of the great outdoors virtually swallows up the human stories, gives them perspective against the enormous monoliths of raw nature. In fact, most Westerns, not just those of John Ford, establish their locations and their moods by opening scenes of either the desert or the stark, snow-covered mountains. Think of *Stagecoach*, *Red River*, *The Searchers*, *High Plains Drifter*, *Pale Rider*, and so many more. It never ceases to amaze me when I drive across states like Kansas, as I do at least twice a year on my way to the mountains, that it was in uninspiring prairies where most of the real stories of the West occurred. Dodge City, Abilene, and Wichita are nowhere near mountains or deserts. At least Deadwood is in the Black Hills of South Dakota and Tombstone

135

in Arizona does have some reasonably impressive hills and desert outside of town.

The film directors corrected the absence of remarkable landscape on retelling the tales. Obviously, they did so, in the first instance to dress up their sets, to make the film more visually exciting for the viewer. But there is much more to their choice of locales than providing us with breathtaking vistas. In the majority of Westerns the setting is in or near a desert. Those opening shots of vast deserts or stark mountains and monoliths, as Tompkins notes, foreshadow the omnipresent theme of the Western: death. "The desert is the landscape of death."[1]

The barren beautiful landscapes are as much characters in the films as any of the humans. The wilderness is the one thing the westerner reveres. J. B. Books tells Mrs. Rogers that he will not accept her invitation to attend church services, because his church has always been the wilderness. He will worship in no other. Joshua Sloan, the ersatz preacher in *The Ballad of Cable Hogue*, remarks in his eulogy for Hogue, "He never went to church. He didn't need to. The whole desert was his cathedral." The wilderness is the one thing with which the westerner seeks identity. And, of course, in the end he generally achieves it.

The landscape also makes clear what the films reject as unworthy: cities, soft people, and soft things, and of course, anything Eastern, anything civilized. As Will Penny tells Catherine Adams, "This is a hard country, double hard." If you want to survive in the West, you must imitate the West itself, its hardness, its bleakness, its unforgiving nature. All of that being true, why in what is his most bitter vision of the death of the West, did John Ford not avail himself of the landscape of death? Why was this typically prevailing character not cast in *The Man Who Shot Liberty Valance*?

The film, like the majority of Westerns, is centrally about death and dying. Unlike most Westerns, it is bleak, interior. It is about a West that is already dead and replaced with flimsy, artificial legend. The film is a funeral, black and gray and dark, all vertical and horizontal planes, shot in deep-focus chiaroscuro. It is also something of a morality play in which the good, as discussed earlier, does something bad in order to do something good. The problem is that what is good and what is bad has gotten twisted and redefined in the process so that there is a genuine ambiguity about what is right and what is wrong and what is left.

The film is set at a funeral, or rather at the undertaker's, as the body of Tom Doniphon is prepared for burial. The highly respected Senator Ransom Stoddard (played by James Stewart) and his wife Hallie (Vera Miles) arrive to pay their last respects. Most of the townsfolk are puzzled as to why the Senator would bother. Doniphon was a drunken bum with no special social or moral standing in the town of Shinbone. Stoddard has been a highly successful politico, rising through the elected ranks to his current position. The local newspaper editor, whose name is Scott, wants the story that explains Stoddard's appearance at the undertaker's and Stoddard, the consummate politician, obliges him. The bulk of the film is a flashback to the early days of Shinbone and the story, as told by Stoddard, of the odd relationship that emerged between Tom Doniphon (played by John Wayne), Stoddard, and Hallie.

Stoddard, an easterner with a law school education, was pulled from the stagecoach that was taking him to Shinbone and severely beaten by the outlaw Liberty Valance. Doniphon finds Stoddard and brings him to his girlfriend Hallie so that she and the Ericsons, who run a restaurant, can nurse him. Throughout most of the flashback Stoddard is shown in light and neutral colors and, importantly, he is almost always in a prone, horizontal, position being looked down upon by Doniphon, Valance, and the other westerners, including Hallie. This is in stark contrast to the opening and closing sequences where he is vertical and straight while it is Doniphon, prone in his pine coffin, who is looked down upon by Stoddard. The film is about that change of positions, from the horizontal to the vertical and vice versa.

Hallie is, arguably, the most interesting character throughout the film. A convincing case can be made that she is the symbol of the West for Ford and that the story is one of her repression, as well as the death of the West, at the hands of the civilizing easterner. At the beginning of the flashback, Hallie is wild, loud-mouthed, and free. She is unafraid to criticize the men. She dresses in light colored dresses, her hair is in pigtails, and she "radiates around the men."[2] As she comes under the influence of Stoddard, however, she is more and more toned down. Her spirit is sapped and when we see her at the end of the film, she is bitter, but resigned. Hallie could not read or write and so she is tutored by Stoddard, but when we see her in his class she already shows signs of the repression of civilization. "Hallie's repression is like that of the West—Ranse's influence 'tames' her, makes her respectable and educated, but takes the fire, freedom, and passion out of her."[3] As Stoddard and his wife are leaving on the train out of Shinbone, their visit completed, Hallie gazes out of the window and, rather laconically but with a distinct edge of bitterness, says to the Senator, "Look at it. It was once a wilderness; now it's a garden. Aren't you proud?" Of course, the sad fact is that he is proud and willing to take the credit. After all, he is a politician. To become that he has, himself, changed. He was once a terrified, inept dude, suited primarily for woman's work, wearing an apron in many of the scenes, including his "shoot-out" with Liberty Valance. Now he has become a heartless, platitude-spouting, superficial politician who cannot even find the right words to say over the coffin to the oldest friends of Doniphon. At his farewell to Pompey, Doniphon's servant who had a great deal to do with getting both Doniphon and Stoddard out of tough situations, all he can do is to slip some money in his hand and say, "pork chop money." Whatever sincerity and verve Stoddard had in the old days, like Hallie's fire, has been extinguished. And so, the West.

II

The film's title is *The Man Who Shot Liberty Valance*. The legend on which the Senator's career was built is that Stoddard was that man. And for a short while he even believed that he had killed Valance. He learns from Doniphon that, from the shadows of an alley, Doniphon had shot Valance with a rifle. Doniphon, the true westerner, killed Liberty: and he did it in a way that violated all of the principles of the westerner. By letting Stoddard take the credit, credit he would not want anyway, Doniphon propels Stoddard into the political limelight, and more important, he seals his own doom. But who really killed Liberty Valance?

The answer is unambiguous. Stoddard killed Liberty even if the bullet from his gun never entered the body of Liberty Valance. The easterner's conception of civilization and law and order, the very idea that the wilderness could and should be converted into a garden, destroyed the West. And with the demise of the conditions the westerner requires to flourish, what was left for Tom Doniphon? His moral compass was shattered. Everything he cared about was destroyed. And so was he. "Tom's progression, from the respectable, capable moral center of the town to a virtual bum, is inversely related to Ranse's progression and in a strange way parallels that of Hallie. He is kindly and jovial in the beginning of the film, very much in control and respected by everyone. What he loses . . . is his personal center."[4]

Doniphon creates a new hero for a new West (Ransom Stoddard) by destroying the West in which he, Doniphon, can comfortably function. That West contains Liberty Valances, Jack Wilsons, Franks, and various and sundry mean and ornery individuals taking too much advantage of the freedom the wilderness offers. As Marshal Thibido, in *The Shootist*, tells Books, they must be weeded out to make the West a "goddamn Garden of Eden." In effect, the westerners must be buried to make things safe for law, order, and civilization.

Doniphon, however, weeds himself out, unknowingly sacrifices him-

self, thinking he is big enough to bear the responsibility for what he has
done. He is not. He cannot be killed off by Stoddard and he has run out of
West into which to ride away. All of that monumental scenery in the other
Ford Westerns is reduced in *The Man Who Shot Liberty Valance* to a single
cactus rose stuck on what is obviously a sound stage, a cactus rose that
Stoddard disparages when he tells Hallie that she will have real roses, the
cultivated, garden-variety type that are put in glass vases in tea rooms.

III

My interpretation of *The Man Who Shot Liberty Valance* is guided in some,
not insignificant, measure by a conversation I had with German scholar
Vittorio Hosle and the reading of an article he and Mark Roche wrote
about the film.[5] Hosle and Roche persuasively find a conceptual structure
for the film in Giambattista Vico's concept of human history. Vico distinguished three ages in the history of every culture: the age of gods, the age
of heroes, and the age of men. Vico writes, "The first nature (in the historical course nations run), by a powerful deceit of imagination . . . was a
poetic or creative nature which we may be allowed to call divine, as it
ascribed to physical things the being of substances animated by gods, assign-
ing the gods to them according to its idea of each . . . The second was
heroic nature . . . They justly regarded their heroism as including the natural nobility in virtue of which they were the princes of the human race . . .
The third was human nature, intelligent and hence modest, benign, and
reasonable, recognizing for laws conscience, reason, and duty."[6] With regard to the customs of each age he tells us, "The first customs were all
tinged with religion and pity . . . The second were choleric and punctilious,
like those related to Achilles. The third are dutiful, taught to everyone by
his own sense of civil duty."[7] With reference to kinds of governments he
says, "The first were divine, or, as the Greeks would say, theocratic . . .
The second were heroic or aristocratic governments which is to say governments of the optimates in the sense of the most powerful . . . The third
are human governments, in which, in virtue of the equality of the intelligent nature which is the proper nature of man, all are accounted equal
under the laws . . ."[8] And the three ages also give rise to three kinds of
characters. Vico writes, "The first were divine . . . The second were heroic
characters, which were also imaginative universals to which they reduced
the various species of heroic things, as to Achilles all deeds of valiant fighters
and to Ulysses all devises of clever men . . . Finally, there were invented (in

the age of men) the vulgar characters which went along with the vulgar languages."[9]

The Man Who Shot Liberty Valance is a film about the transition from the heroic to the nonheroic age of men. The same theme, of course, dominates such films as *Butch Cassidy and the Sundance Kid*, *The Ballad of Cable Hogue*, *The Wild Bunch*, *McCabe and Mrs. Miller*, and the "modern" Westerns such as *Rancho Deluxe*, *Kid Blue*, *Hearts of the West*, *The Good Old Boys*, and *Lonely Are the Brave*. Vico's age of heroes is an age without a civil state, rather like Hobbes's state of nature, though Vico rejects Hobbes's account. It is an age in which physical prowess, force, and violence set the rules of human interactions. In the opening segment of the flashback, as noted in an earlier chapter, while Liberty Valance is flogging Stoddard, he tears up Stoddard's law books and tells him he is giving him a lesson in Western law.

In Vico's age of heroes the duel between two strong men, strong of will and strong in physical force and prowess, is the defining moment of human action. What happens in the duel between Liberty Valance and Ransom Stoddard is a travesty, a mocking of that primary symbol of the heroic age, a sure sign that the age is ending. Its replacement, for Vico, is an age dominated by the rule of law and reason and not physical prowess or force, the age of modern men and their machinery.

Stoddard is the transition figure in *The Man Who Shot Liberty Valance*, hopefully and confidently he preaches and teaches the virtues of the new age, literacy, representative government, equality. It is an age in which he will thrive, paradoxically, because the general public thinks he is heroic and he knows that he is not. Characteristic of the age of men is the rise of public education, facility with language, and, as Hosle and Roche note, "calculating intellect." They write, "The age of men necessarily culminates in what Vico calls the 'barbarism of reflection,' an empty reasoning that has lost any substantial contents, a strategic attitude toward fellow human beings, a lack of roots and traditions and therefore of emotional richness. One aspect of the barbarism of reflection is the spreading of lying."[10]

As noted earlier, westerners hate liars. Lying is an art of language, and language is the tool of the easterner. The westerner says little, and when he does talk he is direct and honest. Vico's age of men is sustained on language and so lies. "The question will no longer be, who is quicker at shooting, but who is better at speaking."[11] In *The Man Who Shot Liberty Valance* nothing is both clearer and more poignant than the hero's, Tom Doniphon's, willingness to allow a lie to be promulgated, a lie on which not only Stoddard's whole career will be based, but one that will destroy both Doniphon and the age of heroes in which he thrives and has moral authority.

We see one particularly pernicious form of civilized lying, characteristic of the new age, in the contrast between the two newspaper editors in the film. Denton Peabody, the courageous editor of the *Shinbone Star* in the flashback, is a champion of the truth. He prints the truth even though it nearly costs him his life. He is an easterner, sent west by Horace Greeley's advice, but he grasps and adopts the westerner's demand for truth and he honors it. Editor Scott, who interviews Senator Stoddard in the beginning and end of the film, is the epitome of the current journalist. He could care less about the truth. What matters to him is the story, and rather than going out to investigate, he prefers to merely report on what people say, usually in staged press conferences. The neat twist in *The Man Who Shot Liberty Valance* is that even after learning the truth from the Senator's confession about who actually shot Liberty, the editor prefers the legend. "This is the West, sir." he says, "When the legend becomes fact, print the legend." The only reason the legend has become fact, of course, is because that is what people want to believe, and the Senator needed them to believe it to achieve his position of power. Furthermore, the most ironic claim of all is "This is the West, sir." It most certainly is not the West, the West died with Liberty Valance and Tom Doniphon. It has become the new East, West only in geographic location relative to the old East, or, rather, it is Vico's age of men, where stories are judged on merits quite other than their truth. What sells to the largest audience is what is worthy of print.

IV

There is a moral, an ethical, depth (to borrow a term from Hosle and Roche) to the westerner hero, to Tom Doniphon, that is almost completely lacking in Ransom Stoddard and absent in those who have followed after him in our civilized age. Doniphon is a suffering servant who makes a hero out of Stoddard at the cost of his own virtue. Doniphon could, we are aware, at any time call out Liberty Valance and, face to face, shoot it out with him. He almost does so in Peter Ericson's restaurant when Liberty trips Stoddard causing him to fall, sending Doniphon's steak to the floor. There is also little doubt that in a duel Doniphon would prevail. Why then does he let Stoddard go out into the street on that dark night to face Valance? Is it perhaps that he recognizes that his time is passing? Or does he want to see if Stoddard is brave enough to face what will surely be his death? I suppose it does not matter, but it does concern me because had Doniphon taken Stoddard's place in a face-to-face duel with Valance, he could have preserved his age for at least a short time longer, perhaps through his life. He could have succeeded in doing something J. B. Books does: saving himself from the new age. But the act he chooses to perform is, I suspect, of a greater ethical value.

Doniphon cold-bloodedly shoots Valance. What makes that so important is that by killing Valance that way, by murdering him, he forever deprives himself of the opportunity to publicly claim the deed. His act does not fit the heroic model so he cannot proclaim it. Instead, the only one who can claim the deed is the bumbling dude with the apron on who had at least enough nerve to face Valance out in the open. By killing Valance in what the hero knows is a cowardly fashion, the hero forfeits his claim to the heroic. Doniphon is well aware of that. Still, it makes sense to say that what he did was perhaps more morally admirable than had he stood out in the light and called out Valance for a face-to-face duel. He not only kills off a bullying threat to the civilizing forces in the town, a force of evil from any perspective, he gives the state a leader versed in the new age's arts of rhetoric and representative government, and with the essential ability to sustain a public career built on a lie. A dirty, unshaven, scruffy-looking Doniphon confronts Stoddard at the statehood convention, when Stoddard is reluctant to accept the nomination to represent the territory in Washington.

> Doniphon: Cold-blooded murder, but I can live with it. Hallie's happy. She wanted you alive.
> Stoddard: But you saved my life.
> Doniphon: I wish I hadn't. Hallie's your girl now. Go back in there and take that nomination. You taught her to read and write, now give her something to read and write about.

Doniphon senses, as we see him in the bar directly after the shooting of Liberty, that he has killed something essential to his own welfare: the West, the land of heroes and death. "With the introduction of legality and the elimination of Liberty (and the forces he symbolizes), the hero becomes superfluous. Tom's killing Liberty consummates the Western in a very specific sense that it renders the hero unnecessary."[12]

Liberty Valance is virtually a caricature of evil in the film. He is played by Lee Marvin in exaggerated stylistic ways. From his flamboyant dress to his bellowing and swaggering and threatening, he is evil personified. You cannot miss it. He proclaims himself the bad guy by everything he does, every move he makes, every word that he utters. If you want to know what is evil in the old Shinbone, there is an unambiguous ostensive answer: Liberty. But where, or who, is evil after Liberty is killed? The moral clarity of the heroic age is muddied in the age of men. Ironically perhaps, the only character in the nonflashback segments of the film who dresses in anything like the distinct whites and blacks favored by Liberty Valance and Tom Doniphon is Senator Stoddard. He wears a black suit and sports a white hat. Doniphon usually wears a black shirt and a white hat. But in the new age, evil is rendered into shades of gray and death has lost its sting.

V

As discussed in chapter 3, the easterner's civilization brings with it the Christian's conception of death. Death is no longer annihilation, and so it is no longer to be greatly feared, in and of itself, as the end of all you are or ever will be. What is to be feared is a tortured afterlife as punishment for a life of sin. Sin avoidance is more important than courageously facing one's death. The death of the West is the death of death. Little wonder that the civilized world ostracizes death. It will not countenance a return of the phantom of the wilderness.

Tom Doniphon's death is not courageous. It is, in fact, pathetic. He died a destitute bum who had sold his guns to buy booze. His figurative death occurred many years before he was finally laid out in the pine coffin in the undertaker's parlor. It occurred on that same night he shot Liberty Valance. He sees Hallie embrace the wounded Stoddard and assumes that means that she is in love with Ranse rather than with him. That he is wrong in that assumption, is, of course, of no consequence for the story. He heads to the bar and gets falling-down drunk. Pompey has to throw him in a buckboard to take him back to his ranch. A little earlier the corpse of Liberty Valance had been thrown into a similar buckboard. The two dominant figures of the heroic age are rendered prone, horizontal, in one evening, and both are unceremoniously carted out of town. The westerner hero takes the same exit as the westerner villain he has banished. Without each other, both are finished. Once they rode horses, now they are carted away in wagons. If they had hung around longer, like Senator Stoddard, they would arrive and depart on a symbol of the age of men, the mechanical age, the train that opens and closes the film. The primitive natural world of the westerner is replaced with machinery.

The theme that machinery marks the death of the West is played over and over again in Westerns. In *The Shootist* one of the gunfighters, Mike Sweeney, arrives at the Metropole in a horseless carriage. Before Books enters, he stops to look at the contraption and shakes his head. When a gunman arrives in an automobile, the West is surely breathing its last. In

The Wild Bunch, the machinery is a machine gun and a car. They have even heard tell of some fellows flying an airplane. The machine gun, and earlier the Gatling gun, depersonalizes the duel and destroys the human confrontational element.

The current run of action films, in which the hero has a machine gun in each hand, does not, to my mind, approach the personal drama of the Western. Skill and prowess is drained from the experience. The hero mows down dozens of the villain's minions. We just want to see him do it. The more the merrier, especially if each scene ends with an explosion and a massive fire. The same is true for the shiny science fiction machines. Attempts have been made to translate the themes and plot lines of Westerns into outer-space settings, but they are dismal failures. The primary reason, I suspect, is that the science fiction setting, by its very nature, cannot be primitive. The old Thirties and Forties cliffhanger, like the ones with Boston Blackie and The Phantom, adapt better to the outer-space settings. The extensive machinery depersonalizes the life-and-death situation.

The machine as the symbol of the age of men—the victory of civilization—is perhaps nowhere better portrayed than in *The Ballad of Cable Hogue*. Cable has fallen in love with Hildy, a prostitute. She, like most prostitutes in Westerns, is driven out of town by the good Christian women and stays for a while with Cable at the way station for the stage coaches he has built by the waterhole he discovered in the desert. Her sights, however, are set on going to San Francisco and marrying a wealthy man. She leaves Cable, but sometime later returns in a chauffeur-driven automobile. She has obviously found her rich man. In fact, she married him and when he died of a stroke, in ecstasy while making love to her, she inherited a fortune. She is going East to live in style and she invites Cable to join her. He is ready to leave his desert, but when the car, driverless while it is being serviced, starts to roll down an incline, he saves the life of his former enemy, the pathetic Samuel Bowen. In the process, however, he is run over and mortally injured. The preacher, Joshua Sloan, in time to preach a eulogy for Cable, arrives on a motorcycle that Cable declares to be an ugly thing, echoing what the stagecoach driver says of Hildy's automobile. The machinery of the age of men does the killing of the westerner, in this case unassisted by a confirmed Christian civilizationist.

Tompkins is right when she tells us that Westerns take place in the West because "the West was a place where technology was primitive, physical conditions harsh, the social infrastructure nonexistent, and the power and presence of women proportionately reduced."[13] She is wrong, however, when she concludes that Westerns are not about the encounter between civilization and the frontier. All of the things she ascribes to the West amount to its essential frontier, or wilderness nature. She is much too ready to categorize Westerns as male attempts to restore their mastery over women to see that she has actually laid her fingers on what the westerner really fears and so what he really cares most about. He fears the destruction of the domain in which he has a morally significant role to play and in which his death, his annihilation, can amount to something. Cable Hogue says as he is dying, "All my life I've been scared of this livin'. Now I've got to do the other." That women in the stories happen typically to be identified with the world view that annihilates death only indicates that they are, as the Western and the westerner sees it, on the winning side. The Western does not offer hope to men in fear of losing their identities to a society dominated by women. Just the opposite. Tom Doniphon dies a bum whom almost everyone in Shinbone has forgotten. McCabe dies forgotten in a snowdrift. Most of the others ride off into the mountains or the desert with little or no hope and death waiting at every bend of the river.

And further, in *The Man Who Shot Liberty Valance*, it is a man, not a woman, who corrupts the West with civilization. Hallie is herself corrupted and repressed by Stoddard. She sacrifices her relationship with Doniphon, she loved him and never stopped loving him, to marry Stoddard. We have some hints that she regrets her choice. She is cold to the Senator both when they arrive in Shinbone and when they leave. She is responsible for placing the cactus rose on the coffin, and she wants to return to Shinbone and leave the Washington power circle. She has personally undergone the transition of the West, and it is a painful experience. We can only wonder if she is also in on the great lie, the lie that Stoddard feels finally compelled to reveal to the newspaper editor. Would he tell him, and, therefore, likely the whole world, and not have told her? When the conductor at the end of the film says to Stoddard, "Nothing's too good for the man who shot Liberty Valance," Hallie vaguely sighs and turns away from Stoddard. If he did tell her, then she should have realized that the man who really needed her love is the man who has lost everything. And that is not Stoddard.

Stoddard in the beginning of the film appears to be the weakling. As previously noted, he is almost always in a prone position vis-a-vis the other major characters. They all loom over him, including Hallie. But Stoddard's position turns out to be a deception. He would have been strong enough on his own to move up the political ladder. After the early stages of nursing him back to health, he does not really need Hallie. But Doniphon needs her, and, some might say, he has earned her by sacrificing himself by shooting Liberty Valance. She, apparently, does not recognize this at the crucial time and, we see from her actions when she arrives to pay respects to his corpse, that she regrets her failure.

VI

The "transition Westerns" depict the loss of the West, the death of the West, and the ascension to dominance of Vico's modern age of men and machines—the industrial civilization that the westerner associates with the East. A similar transition was depicted by Aeschylus in the *Oresteia*, a point noted by Hosle and Roche.[14] But there is a very major difference between the transition Western and the *Oresteia*: the latter provides its audience with an optimistic, even congratulatory conclusion. There is an air of "look what we have done, isn't it great" about the trilogy. The transition from the world of blood vengeance to law and justice is depicted as a major accomplishment, and there is no sense of nostalgia to return to the good old days of wives killing husbands, fathers sacrificing daughters, sons murdering mothers, and whole societies decimated by civil war. The transition from a society driven by passion and revenge to one operating according to the dictates of reason was celebrated as a significant improvement. The third play in the trilogy, *The Eumenides*, ends, however, with an integration of the old with the new. The Furies, the old goddesses, are not totally dismissed from the system of justice that replaces the old order. They are changed by and for it.

> Furies: All's lost, our ancient powers torn away by their cunning, ruthless hands, the gods so hard to wrestle down obliterate us all.
> Athena: No, I will never tire of telling you your gifts, so that you, the older gods, can never say that I, a young god, and the mortals of my city drove you outcast, outlawed from the land . . .
> Leader of the Furies: And you will pledge me that, for all time to come?
> Athena: Yes—I must never promise things I cannot do.
> Leader of the Furies: Your magic is working . . . I can feel the hate, the fury slip away.
> Athena: At last! And now take root in the land and win yourself new friends.[15]

In the transition Westerns like *The Man Who Shot Liberty Valance*, there is little optimism about the new age. There is mostly a deep sense of loss, perpetuated by a vague sort of nostalgia for the former age of heroes. There is no sense that it was paradise lost, but it was a time of clearer moral distinctions, and a time when passion was not sucked out of the system by rules and laws and formal education in reading, writing, and civics. Even Senator Stoddard feels the loss, though probably not as much as does Hallie. In a flat-affected way she tells the Senator, "My roots are here. I guess my heart is here. Yes, let's come back." But it sounds as if she knows that she can't go home again. In her case, home is not there anymore. The train may stop in the new Shinbone, but only a stagecoach that is now a relic in cobwebs once traveled to the Shinbone that was her home. Modernity, the age of men, has changed it all. The heroes are now dead and buried and forgotten. Well, all are dead and buried except the one who is a phony: her husband. When the conductor says that fateful final line to the Stoddards as the train leaves Shinbone, "Nothing's too good for the man who shot Liberty Valance," the cringing inside Stoddard is felt by all of us. "Not only is the Senator disturbed by the fact that the merit of another person is ascribed to him (he cannot, for example, light his pipe), he also finally grasps that not only his existence, but the age of men as a whole is based on a lie."[16]

Josh, in *The Ballad of Cable Hogue*, emphasizes once again the westerner's hatred of the lie in his eulogy for Cable. He says to God:

> Josh: Now most funeral orations lie about a man, compare him to the angels, whitewash him with a really wide brush. But you know, Lord, and I know, that it is just not true. Now a man is made out of bad as well as good, all of us. Cable Hogue was born into this world, nobody knows when or where. He came stumbling out of the wilderness like a prophet of old. Out of the barren wastes, he carved himself a one-man kingdom. Some said he was ruthless . . . But you could do worse, Lord, than to take to your bosom Cable Hogue. He wasn't really a good man. He wasn't a bad man. But, Lord, he was a man . . .

Stoddard's eulogy will be dominated by the lie that he was the man who shot Liberty Valance. Doniphon may have thought he could live with having committed cold-blooded murder. He was wrong. But Stoddard has lived the lie, and he has prospered. The age of men has made living the lie far easier than the age of heroes would permit living with cold-blooded murder.

VII

The motion picture is a perfect medium in which to depict the transition between these ages of Vico. Novels and poems fall far short of the film. The reason is that the transition is most evident in the distinction between language-using and action. Those of the heroic age, as noted earlier, are not talkers. Most are not even literate. Pea Eye Parker, in *Streets of Laredo*, is married to Lorena. She is a schoolteacher, but Pea has mastered only two letters, P and Y. Tom Doniphon can barely read; Hallie can neither read nor write until she becomes Stoddard's pupil. Will Penny is not literate. The list could go on. But literacy, or rather the lack of it, is only part of the story. The westerners reject talking in favor of body language and actions. They communicate in gestures, usually very subtle ones: a wink, a grimace, a nod, a scowl, even a smile. A study of Clint Eastwood's "Man With No Name" series of films would undoubtedly provide an adequate primer on the westerner's use of such facial expressions. He runs through most of them in the first five minutes of *A Fistful of Dollars*. In the medium of film the juxtaposition of these two forms of communication, nonverbal and verbal, can be brought out in touching clarity. The film shows what words cannot tell: there can be deep bonds of understanding between people who don't talk to each other very much.

The modern age is the age of the talker, where talking is assimilated to acting and where philosophers have spent the better part of a century analyzing language as if it were the most important part of human life. If only we could understand reference, speech acts, language games, and semantic meaning, we would grasp the essence of relationships between humans and between humans and the world! Doniphon tells Stoddard, "You talk too much, think too much." Sometimes the mere placement of a cactus rose can convey so much more than all of one's attempts to verbalize how much was lost and how inferior the new age might be to the good old days. But such communication only occurs between the worn-out survivors of the former nonverbal age. In *The Man Who Shot Liberty Valance*, Hallie, Link Appleyard, and Pompey grasp the message, but there must remain doubt as to whether the Senator "gets it." On the train, after he does not respond to Hallie's "Aren't you proud?" Stoddard asks, "Hallie, who put the cactus roses on Tom's coffin?" She simply and flatly responds, "I did." He says no more. Why did he ask?

The transition Westerns take us "west of everything." They all end with death. What is of some interest is the types of deaths that are portrayed. The Wild Bunch, J. B. Books, Butch Cassidy and the Sundance Kid go out with their boots on and guns blazing. But all, in different ways, are killed by their inferiors. Books is shot in the back by the bartender. Pike is shot by a prostitute and a young boy in a soldier suit, reminiscent of the opening shot of the children feeding the scorpions to the killer ants. Butch and Sundance are gunned down by what looks to be a major segment of the nondescript Bolivian army. None of their killers are their equals. Butch and Sundance throughout their getaway fear that they are being tracked by the famous scout LeFors. He would be worthy of them. In their last moments alive in Bolivia, they convince themselves that LeFors is not in the army that surrounds them and so they have hope of survival. Pike should be killed by someone of the stature of Thornton, not by a Mexican whore and a boy playing soldier. But the end of the age does not go out with a bang. Tom Doniphon dies a drunken bum whose boots have been stolen by the undertaker, and Cable Hogue is run over by a driverless automobile. Only Doniphon is killed by someone worthy of his stature. He is killed by himself, but even then he is but a mere shell of the man who shot Liberty Valance.

The last twenty minutes of *McCabe and Mrs. Miller* provide a stunning visualization of the death of the West and the transition to the new age. McCabe, a gambler, and Mrs. Miller, a prostitute who has become the madam of McCabe's whorehouse, have successfully exploited the citizens of the mining and lumbering town of Presbyterian Church, named for the church whose steeple dominates the town. A corporation, represented by Sears and Hollander, wants to buy out McCabe's interests in his various businesses. Because he is woefully unskilled in negotiating on a corporate level, he insults them, and they send three killers to permanently put him out of the way. The culmination of the film involves two interlinked events in the small town: the stalking of McCabe by the three killers and the town's attempt to put out a fire that threatens to burn down the church. Both happen in a heavy snowfall.

McCabe had entered the church to evade the killers and to use the steeple to get a better idea of where they were. When he descends the steeple, he is confronted by the minister who has taken McCabe's shotgun. The minister throws McCabe out of the church, a building he has never entered previously for the purposes for which it was constructed. One of the killers, Butler, bursts into the church, mistakes the minister, who is holding McCabe's shotgun, for his quarry, and kills him. As he dies, the minister drops the kerosene lantern he has just lit, and it starts the church on fire. The townspeople, oblivious to the life-and-death battle on their streets, discover the church is on fire and rush to get buckets and a steam engine from which they will drain water to douse the flames. The machinery chugs intermittently through the scene as it provides water to save the church. The imagery is obvious, modern machinery saves religion. However, the concerted efforts of the various and sundry folks of the town, including a brigade of prostitutes, has much to do with the successful quashing of the fire. In any event, the church is saved and there is much rejoicing.

McCabe manages to kill off all three of the assassins, but he is mortally gut shot and he dies, frozen, in a deep snowdrift, totally unnoticed by the town. Mrs. Miller drifts off into an opium reverie in the Chinese lodgings.

It is hardly a triumph for McCabe, but it is one for both the town and the church that aptly share the same name. Perhaps the one saving grace for the westerner is that he is swallowed up by brutal nature until he is virtually indistinguishable from the virgin snow. The saved church offers salvation and life everlasting—the death of death—to its new, modern-age parishioners. The dead westerner is simply dead and gone. Indeed, his presence, and even any memory of him, is being erased both by nature itself and by the opium Mrs. Miller languidly smokes.

NOTES

1. Tompkins, *West of Everything*, 70.
2. J. A. Place, *The Western Films of John Ford* (Secaucus, N.J., 1974), 220.
3. Ibid.
4. Ibid., 223–24.
5. Mark W. Roche and Vittorio Hosle, "Vico's Age of Heroes and the Age of Men in John Ford's Film, *The Man Who Shot Liberty Valance*," *Clio* 23, no. 2 (1993): 131–47.
6. T. G. Bergin and M. Fisch, *The New Science of Giambattista Vico* (Ithaca, N.Y., 1968), 336.
7. Ibid., 337.
8. Ibid., 339.
9. Ibid., 341.
10. Roche and Hosle, "Vico's Age of Heroes and the Age of Men in John Ford's Film, *The Man Who Shot Liberty Valance*," 133.
11. Ibid., 138.
12. Ibid., 143.
13. Tompkins, *West of Everything*, 44–45.
14. Roche and Hosle, "Vico's Age of Heroes and the Age of Men in John Ford's Film, *The Man Who Shot Liberty Valance*," 135.
15. Aeschylus, *The Oresteia*, trans. by R. Fagles (New York, 1979), 269–71.
16. Roche and Hosle, "Vico's Age of Heroes and the Age of Men in John Ford's Film, *The Man Who Shot Liberty Valance*," 139.

AFTERWORD

Where does all of this fixation on death as annihilation lead with respect to ethics in Westerns? I think it is of secondary, but still important, interest that the ethics that emerges is *not*, in most respects, the ethics typically identified as masculine in the recent philosophical literature, where a contrast is usually drawn between a masculine ethics of rules and principles focused on contract and justice and a feminine ethics of care and kindness focused on relationships between people. The Western scrambles the categories.

The Western's ethics are not antithetical to caring and kindness for others, but it doles them out only as and when warranted in accord with what comes close to an Aristotelian account of friendship. Of note in the *Nicomachean Ethics* is that the perfect kind of friendship is described as a rare thing that can be extended from a person to a partner only after "each partner has impressed the other that he is worthy of affection, and until each has won the other's confidence."[1] Such perfect friendship is not to be indiscriminately tendered to the meek, the peacemakers, and the other subjects of the Christian Beatitudes. In the Western, a comparable understanding of real friendship is played out in hundreds of plots. The crucial concepts are understood in terms of demonstrable worth and confidence. Recall Josey Wales's "I rode with him; I got no complaints."

The ethics of the Western places very high value on independence, pride, loyalty, friendship or camaraderie, honor, self-reliance, valor, and, most important, vengeance and moral (righteous) hatred. Each of those concepts needs to be explicated in the context of the Western, and I will take up that task in a subsequent work. The westerner is relatively tolerant and is certainly not a social reformer. But circumstances do arise when the Western ethic requires him to take a stand. As Randolph Scott says in *The Tall T*, "There's some things a man can't ride around." What falls in that category defines, in large measure, the ethics of Westerns and the virtues of vengeance.

NOTES

1. Aristotle, *Nicomachean Ethics*, 1156b.

151

BIBLIOGRAPHY

BOOKS

Aeschylus. *The Oresteia*, trans. R. Fagles. New York: Penguin Books, 1979.

Aquinas, St. Thomas. *Summa Theologica*, trans. The Fathers of the English Dominican Province. London, 1912.

Aristotle. *Nicomachean Ethics*, trans. M. Ostwald. Indianapolis: Bobbs Merrill, 1962.

Aristotle. *Poetics*, trans. P. Wheelwright, in *Wheelwright's Aristotle*. New York: Odyssey Press, 1935.

Augustine, St. *The City of God*, trans. Walsh, Zema, Monahan, and Honan. Garden City: Prentice Hall, 1958.

Austen, Jane. *Pride and Prejudice*. 1813. Franklin Center, PA: Franklin Publishing, 1980.

Austin, J. L. *Philosophical Papers*. 2d ed, 1970. Oxford: Oxford University Press, 1961.

Benjamin, Martin. *Splitting the Difference*. Lawrence: University Press of Kansas, 1990.

Bergin, T. G. and M. Fisch. *The New Science of Giambattista Vico*. Ithaca, NY: Cornell University Press, 1968.

Bolt, Robert. *A Man For All Seasons*. New York: French, 1962.

Bowra, C. W. *The Greek Experience*. New York: Mentor Books, 1959.

Bradley, F. H. *Ethical Studies*. 1876. Oxford: Oxford University Press, 1989.

Burke, James. *The Day the Universe Changed*. London: London Writers Ltd., 1985.

Butler, Joseph. *Fifteen Sermons*. London, 1726.

Choron, Jacques. *Death and Western Thought*. New York: Collier Books, 1963.

Descartes, Rene. *Discourse on Method and Meditations*, trans. L. Lafleur. Indianapolis: Bobbs-Merrill, 1960.

Feldman, Fred. *Confrontations with the Reaper.* New York: Oxford University Press, 1992.

Flanagan, Owen. *Varieties of Moral Personality.* Cambridge, MA: Harvard University Press, 1991.

Frankel, Hermann. *Early Greek Poetry and Philosophy*, trans. Hadas and Willis. New York: Harcourt Brace, 1973.

Frankfurt, Harry. *The Importance Of What We Care About.* Cambridge: Cambridge University Press, 1988.

French, Peter. *Exploring Philosophy.* Cambridge, MA: Schenkmen Publishing, 1970.

————. *Responsibility Matters.* Lawrence, KS: University Press of Kansas, 1992.

————. "The Survival of My Counterpart." *Southern Journal of Philosophy*, 20, no. 1, 1981: 53–60.

French, Philip. *Westerns.* rev. ed. New York: Oxford University Press, 1977.

Halfon, Mark. *Integrity.* Philadelphia: Temple University Press, 1989.

Harrington, Alan. *The Immortalist.* Millbrae, CA: Celestial Arts Publishing, 1977.

Heidel, Alexander. *The Gilgamesh Epic and the Old Testament Parallels.* Chicago: University of Chicago Press, 1946.

Homer. *The Odyssey.* trans. E.V. Rieu. New York: Penguin Books, 1950.

Homer. *The Iliad.* trans. E.V. Rieu. New York: Penguin Books, 1950.

Ireneaus, St. *Adversus Haereses.* trans. D.J. Unger. New York: Paulist Press, 1992.

Kant, Immanuel. *Critique of Practical Reason.* trans. L. W. Beck. Chicago: University of Chicago Press, 1949. Originally published in German, 1788.

————. *The Doctrine of Virtue.* trans. M. Gregor. Philadelphia: University of Pennylvania Press, 1964.

————. *Lectures on Ethics.* trans. L. Infield. New York: Harper and Row, 1963.

Kearl, Michael. *Endings.* New York: Oxford University Press, 1989.

Kekes, John. *Facing Evil.* Princeton: Princeton University Press, 1990.

Kipling, Rudyard. *The One Volume Kipling.* Garden City: Doubleday, Doran and Company, 1932.

L'Amour, Louis. *Hondo.* New York: Bantam Books, 1953.

Lewis, David. "Counterparts of Persons and Their Bodies." *Journal of Philosophy* 68 (1971): 203–11.

Locke, John. *Second Treatise of Government.* 1714.

Lynd, Helen Merrell. *On Shame and the Search for Identity.* New York: John Wiley and Sons, 1967.

Machiavelli, Nicolo. *The Prince.* trans. David Wootton. Indianapolis: Hackett Publishing, 1995.

MacIntyre, Alasdair. *After Virtue.* Notre Dame: University of Notre Dame Press, 1984.

———. *A Short History of Ethics.* New York: Macmillan Publishing, 1966.

Melden, A.I. (ed). *Essays in Moral Philosophy.* Seattle: University of Washington Press, 1958.

Midgley, Mary. *Wickedness.* London: Routledge, 1984.

Milton, John. *Paradise Lost.* 1667.

Montaigne, Michel de. *Essays.* trans. J.M. Cohen. New York: Penguin Books, 1958.

Montet, Pierre. *Everyday Life in Egypt in the Days of Rameses the Great,* trans. A.R. Maxwell-Hyslop and M.S. Drower. Westport, CT: Greenwood Press, 1974.

Munitz, Milton (ed). *Identity and Individuation.* New York: New York University Press, 1971.

Murphy, Jeffrie & Hampton, Jean. *Forgiveness and Mercy.* Cambridge: Cambridge University Press, 1988.

Murray, Gilbert. *Stoic, Christian and Humanist.* London: Allen and Unwin, 1940.

Nietzsche, Friedrich. *Beyond Good and Evil.* trans. W. Kaufmann. New York: Random House, 1966.

Nozick, Robert. *Anarchy, State, and Utopia.* New York: Basic Books, 1974.

Oates, W.J. (ed). *The Stoic and Epicurean Philosophers.* New York: Random House, 1940.

Obayashi, Hiroshi. *Death and Afterlife.* Westport, CT: Greenwood Press, 1992.

Pears, David. "Aristotle's Analysis of Courage," *Midwest Studies in Philosophy* 3 (1978): 273–85.

Peckinpah, Sam. "Interview," *Playboy,* August 1972.

Place, J.A. *The Western Films of John Ford.* Secaucus, NJ: Citadel Press, 1974.

Plato. *The Phaedo.* trans. H. Tredennick. In *The Collected Dialogues of Plato,* ed. Hamilton and Cairns. Princeton: Princeton University Press, 1961.

Pompanazzi, Pietro. "On the Immortality of Man." In *The Renaissance Philosophy of Man.* Chicago: University of Chicago Press, 1950.

Rawls, John. *A Theory of Justice.* Cambridge, MA: Harvard University Press, 1971.

Roche, Mark, and Vittorio Hosle. "Vico's Age of Heroes and the Age of Man in John Ford's Film, *The Man Who Shot Liberty Valance.*" *Clio,* 23, 2 (1993): 131–147.

Rolleston, T.W. *Myths and Legends of the Celtic Race.* New York: Lemma Publishing, 1986.

Ross, David. *Aristotle.* London: Metheun, 1923.

Strawson, Peter. "Freedom and Resentment." *Proceedings of the British Academy* 48 (1962): 1–25.

Taylor, Gabriele. "Integrity." *Proceedings of the Aristotelian Society* 55 (1981): 143–59.

———. *Pride, Shame, and Guilt.* Oxford: Oxford University Press, 1985.

Taylor, Richard. "The Virtue of Pride." In *Reflective Wisdom: Richard Taylor on Issues that Matter,* ed. J. Donnelly. Buffalo: Prometheus Press, 1989.

Tompkins, Jane. *West of Everything.* Oxford: Oxford University Press, 1992.

Tuska, Jon. *The American West in Film.* Westport, CT: Greenwood Press, 1985.

Ullmann, Walter. *The Individual and Society.* Baltimore: Johns Hopkins University Press, 1966.

Walzer, Michael. "Political Action: The Problem of Dirty Hands." *Philosophy and Public Affairs* (1973–74): 160–80.

Weber, Max. "Politics as a Vocation." In *From Max Weber: Essays in Sociology,* trans. H. Gerth and C.W. Mills. New York: Oxford University Press, 1946.

———. *The Protestant Ethic and the Spirit of Capitalism.* trans. T. Parsons. New York: Scribner, 1958.

Winch, Peter. *Ethics and Action.* London: Routledge, 1972.

Wittgenstein, Ludwig. *On Certainty.* trans. D. Paul and G.E.M. Anscombe. Oxford: Basil Blackwell, 1969.

———. *Philosophical Investigations.* trans. G.E.M. Anscombe. London: Macmillan, 1953.

———. *Tractatus Logico Philosophicus.* trans. D.F. Pears and B.F. McGuinness. London: Routledge, 1961.

WESTERNS WATCHED

Films to which reference is made in the book:

Title, Year of Release, Director (Production Company)

The Ballad of Cable Hogue. 1970 Sam Peckinpah (Warner Brothers)

Bend in the River. 1952 Anthony Mann (Universal)

The Big Country. 1958 William Wyler (United Artists/Worldwide)

Butch Cassidy and the Sundance Kid. 1969 George Roy Hill (TCF/Campanile)

Conagher. 1991 Reynaldo Villalobos (Turner)

Cowboy. 1958 Delmer Daves (Columbia)

The Cowboys. 1971 Mark Rydell (Sanford Productions/Warner Brothers)

Dances With Wolves. 1990 Kevin Costner (TIG Productions)

Dead Man's Walk. 1996 Yves Simoneau (Saria Company, Inc and DePasse Enternainment and Larry Levinson Productions)

El Dorado. 1967 Howard Hawks (Laurel)

A Fistful of Dollars. 1964 Sergio Leone (Jolly Film/Constantin/Ocean)

The Good Old Boys. 1995 Tommy Lee Jones (Turner)

The Good, The Bad, and The Ugly. 1966 Sergio Leone (Produzioni Europee Associate/IT)

Hearts of the West. 1975 Howard Zieff (MGM)

High Noon. 1952 Fred Zinnemann (United Artists)

High Plains Drifter. 1972 Clint Eastwood (Malpaso/Universal)

Hombre. 1967 Martin Ritt (20th Century Fox)

Hondo. 1953 John Farrow (Wayne-Fellows)

Johnny Guitar. 1954 Nicholas Ray (Republic)

Kid Blue. 1973 James Frawley (Marvin Schwarz Productions)

Lonely Are the Brave. 1962 David Miller (Universal/Joel)

Lonesome Dove. 1989 Simon Wincer (Motown Production in Association with Wittliff/Pangaea and RHI Entertainment, Inc.)

The Magnificent Seven. 1960 John Sturges (United Artists/Mirisch)

The Man from Laramie. 1955 Anthony Mann (Columbia)

The Man Who Shot Liberty Valance. 1962 John Ford (Ford Productions/Paramount)

Man of the West. 1958 Anthony Mann (Ashton Productions)

McCabe and Mrs. Miller. 1971 Robert Altman (Warner Brothers)

The Missouri Breaks. 1976 Arthur Penn (EK)

Monte Walsh. 1970 William A. Fraker (Cinema Centre Films)

My Darling Clementine. 1946 John Ford (20th Century Fox)

The Naked Spur. 1953 Anthony Mann (MGM)

Once Upon a Time in the West. 1968 Sergio Leone (Rafran Cinematografica/ San Marco)

The Outlaw Josey Wales. 1976 Clint Eastwood (Malpaso)

The Ox-Bow Incident. 1943 William Wellman (20th Century Fox)

The Plainsman. 1936 Cecil B. DeMille (Paramount)

Paint Your Wagon. 1969 Joshua Logan (Paramount)

Pale Rider. 1985 Clint Eastwood (Malpaso)

The Quick and the Dead. 1987 Stephen Dorff (Lorimar)

Rancho Deluxe. 1974 Frank Perry (EK)

Red River. 1948 Howard Hawks (Monterey)

Ride the High Country. 1962 Sam Peckinpah (MGM)

Riders of the Purple Sage. 1996 Charles Haid (Rosemount Productions International in Association with Amer Productions and Zeke Productions)

Rio Bravo. 1959 Howard Hawks (Armada Productions)

The Searchers. 1956 John Ford (Warner Brothers)

Shane. 1953 George Stevens (Paramount)

The Shootist. 1976 Don Siegel (Dino DeLaurentis Corp.)

Stagecoach. 1939 John Ford (Walter Wanger Productions)

Streets of Laredo. 1995 Joseph Sargent (DePasse Entertainment and Larry Levinson Productions in Association with RHI Entertainment, Inc.)

Tall in the Saddle. 1944 Edwin L. Marin (RKO)

The Tall T. 1957 Budd Boetticher (Columbia)

Unforgiven. 1992 Clint Eastwood (Malpaso)

Waterhole #3. 1967 William Graham (Geoffrey Productions)

Welcome to Hard Times. 1967 Burt Kennedy (Max E. Youngstein-David Karr Productions)

The Wild Bunch. 1969 Sam Peckinpah (Warner Brothers)

Will Penny. 1967 Tom Gries (Paramount)

Winchester '73. 1950 Anthony Mann (Universal)

INDEX

159

Ride the High Country, 81, 99–100
Riders of the Purple Sage (1996), 40, 42, 44, 85
Rio Bravo, 121
Robards, Jason, 47, 51
Roche, Mark, 139, 140, 141, 146
Ross, David, 119–20
Rule, Janice, 111
Russell, Bertrand, 29
Ryan, Robert, 68

Scandinavian saga, 94
Scott, Randolph, 32, 69, 76, 151
The Searchers, viii, x, 17, 22, 23, 28, 40, 52, 58, 76, 82, 86, 92, 113, 125, 126, 135
self-respect, 21–23, 96
Seneca, 68, 69
Sermon on the Mount, 15, 18–30, 67
shame, 99–103; and honor, 99–100, 101; and pride, 99–103; and self-alienation, 101;
community-focused, 100–101; personal (self)-focused, 101–103
Shane, vii, viii, 16, 21, 22, 28, 32, 39, 40, 41, 42–43, 44, 45, 55, 77, 78, 79, 80, 82, 85–86, 87, 88, 92, 94, 97, 102, 103, 113, 115, 116, 117, 118, 119, 120, 122, 123, 124, 125, 129
The Shootist, viii, 16, 17, 27–28, 40, 65, 66, 87, 94, 99, 103, 107–32, 135, 138, 142, 143, 148
Sophocles, 78–79
Stagecoach, viii, 17, 25, 39, 69, 121, 135
Stewart, James, 16, 114, 126, 136
Strawson, Peter, 21
Streets of Laredo, 1, 25, 29, 135, 147

Tall in the Saddle, 15
The Tall T, 16, 31, 44, 69, 76, 97, 151
Taylor, Gabriele, 97, 100, 103, 126, 128
Taylor, Richard, 96
Ten Commandments, 30
Tompkins, Jane, viii, ix, 3, 11, 14, 15,

16, 31, 32, 51, 71, 75, 83, 88, 89, 92, 119, 136, 144–45
Tragedy, 75–83; Christian, 80–83; Greek, 75–80
tragic hero, 77
Tuska, Jon, viii–ix

Unforgiven, viii, 17, 23, 25, 28, 70, 79, 82, 87, 89, 112, 114, 115, 125, 126, 132
Urmson, J.O., 122–25

vengeance: as a morally desirable goal, 114–15, 125–26, 151
Vico, Giambattista, 139, 140, 141, 146, 147; and the ages of history of every culture,
139–41
vocation, 34–35

Walzer, Michael, 90, 91, 92
Waterhole #3, 27
Wayne, John, 15, 17, 18, 26, 27, 51, 53, 91, 107, 115, 121, 137
weakness of will, 6–10
Weber, Max, 37, 92
Welcome to Hard Times, 110–11
The Wild Bunch, 84, 115, 126, 128, 140, 144, 148
Will Penny, viii, 16, 18, 31, 32, 42, 47–8, 50, 51, 64, 65, 79, 82, 94, 102, 135, 148
Winch, Peter, 129
Winchester '73, 114
Wittgenstein, Ludwig, 9, 70, 89
women in westerns, 16–23, 30, 32, 39–45; two types of, 17; as communitarians, 23; as feudal Christians, 39; as individualistic Christians, 40–1; and language, 32–33
world views, 3–5, 8,9,11; and beliefs, 4; and ways of life, 9, 11; and what we care about, 5–11; with respect to death, 54–61

ABOUT THE AUTHOR

PETER A. FRENCH is the Marie E. and Leslie Cole Chair in Ethics and Professor of Philosophy at the University of South Florida. He is the Director of The Ethics Center and Chair of the Department of Philosophy of the University of South Florida. He was the Lennox Distinguished Professor of the Humanities and Professor of Philosophy at Trinity University in San Antonio, Texas. He has taught at the University of Northern Arizona; the University of Minnesota; and Dalhousie University, Nova Scotia; and served as Exxon Distinguished Research Professor in the Center for the Study of Values at the University of Delaware. He has a B.A. from Gettysburg College, an M.A. from the University of Southern California, and a Ph.D. from the University of Miami.

Dr. French is the author of sixteen books, including *Corporate Ethics*, *Responsibility Matters*, *Corporations in the Moral Community*, *Collective and Corporate Responsibility*, *Ethics in Government*, and *The Scope of Morality*.

Dr. French is the senior editor of *Midwest Studies in Philosophy*, editor of the *Journal of Social Philosophy*, and was general editor of the *Issues in Contemporary Ethics* series. He has published numerous articles in the major philosophical and legal journals and reviews, many of which have been anthologized.